THE ENGAGEMENT RING

THE
ENGAGEMENT
RING

PRACTICAL LEADERSHIP SKILLS
FOR ENGAGING YOUR EMPLOYEES

LEE ANN POND

LIONCREST

PUBLISHING

THE ENGAGEMENT RING

Practical Leadership Skills for Engaging Your Employees

ISBN 978-1-5445-0624-1 *Hardcover*
      978-1-5445-0623-4 *Paperback*
      978-1-5445-0622-7 *Ebook*

*This book is dedicated to all the "Rogers" who
want to be good leaders and to all of the employees
depending on their "Roger" for good leadership.*

CONTENTS

INTRODUCTION

If there is a book that you want to read, but it hasn't been written yet, then you must write it.

—TONI MORRISON

I've been looking for this book for a long time.

As a nineteen-year-old assistant manager at Baskin Robbins, I received my first taste of being a leader. I was promoted to manage my former peers and tried to navigate being their boss, yet remaining their friend. I'm not sure I did either very well.

I have had both "good" and "bad" leaders through the years. I tried to model my "boss" behavior on what I saw the good bosses do—and tried never to do what the bad bosses did.

But I never really knew what it took to be a great leader and how I was measuring up.

I earned a business degree and went on for an MBA. In all those classes, leadership was still a mystery.

I read every leadership book and article I could get my hands on. I took hours of leadership classes. I would come back to the office pumped up, inspired by what I learned, ready to be a great leader. But, then the realization hit— how do I really do it?

There was a lot of leadership theory in those classes and books, but no specific steps. What is the first thing I should do? And, how would I know I was successfully leading?

Having spent the last fifteen years in the corporate "C" suite, with authority over several departments including human resources, I was ultimately responsible to make sure the entire workforce had good bosses in place. Developing programs to train those leaders led me to the concept of employee engagement.

Then the realization hit—the endgame of leadership is *engaging your followers*!

What does employee engagement have to do with leadership? Well, if you don't have followers, are you a leader? Leadership doesn't exist in a vacuum. Followers are a required component. Engaged followers are the ideal.

Studying the common questions used in employee engagement surveys, the elements required to obtain a positive response on every one of those questions became clear. And *The Engagement Ring* was born!

This book details actionable skills and techniques needed to engage your employees. Not only does it give you the specific steps, but it also conveniently sums them up in a diagram and checklist at the end of the book!

If you follow the steps in *The Engagement Ring*, not only will you be able to increase engagement in your staff, you will become a better leader, manager, and supervisor.

In other words, you will be a good boss.

So, read on!

EMPLOYEE ENGAGEMENT

The secret of successful managing is to keep the five guys who hate you away from the four guys who haven't made up their minds.

—CASEY STENGEL

THE BOSS IS TO BLAME

Would you like your boss to be fired? No? Well, statistics show that one out of three of your employees would like *you* to be fired!

In fact, they would forgo their annual raise if it could happen this year. And, by the way, half of your employees are looking for another job right now.

Shocked? Well, those are the statistics on how employees feel when they are not engaged at work. Offered a better boss or a pay raise, studies show that 35 percent wanted the better boss. Other benefits such as pay, time off, flexible schedules, and retirement plans can cause a slight increase in engagement, but these have been shown to be temporary.

Gallup is the leader in data on employee engagement, and they report that unengaged employees cost $550 billion a year in extra sick days and lost productivity to U.S. corporations.[1]

They have also found that only 30 percent of U.S. employees are engaged at work and 70 percent of an individual's engagement score is based on the employee's relationship with their direct supervisor. Their statistics showed that engaged organizations have 21 percent more profitability and 41 percent less absenteeism.

---

1   Susan Sorenson and Keri Garman, "How to Tackle U.S. Employees' Stagnating Engagement," Gallup, August 5, 2019, https://news.gallup.com/businessjournal/162953/tackle-employees-stagnating-engagement.aspx.

WHO'S ROCKING YOUR BOAT?

Taking Gallup's findings even further, if you filled a row-boat with ten employees from any U.S. organization, there would be two engaged employees upfront, rowing toward the organization's mission. In the middle would be five employees unengaged, not rowing, and there would be two in the back actively disengaged, rowing against the engaged employees in the front.

What can you do? With the two in the back, it's easy. Actively disengaged employees are undermining what their engaged coworkers accomplish. They are disruptive to the organization and need to be given corrective action and possibly fired.

With the 50 percent of your employees who are unengaged in the middle of the rowboat, the answer is not as easy, but it has the most potential to change an organization. These employees are not being disruptive and they are meeting the minimum requirements of their job description.

The problem is, they are just sleepwalking through their day. They are doing the bare minimum on their jobs because their heart isn't in it. They are watching the clock and checking social media whenever they can sneak it in. They dread Monday mornings, maybe even sitting in their cars for a few extra minutes, before walking in with a sinking feeling in their stomach to begin their workweek.

These 50 percent of employees don't feel connected to the organization, don't see how their job moves the organization's mission forward—and in fact probably don't even know what the mission is. They have no real relationship with their boss and don't feel like he or she knows or even cares about them as a person.

They don't feel a sense of team or a feeling of belonging. They feel distant from what may be going on overall in the organization and are isolated, not knowing if they are doing good or bad work, until their annual performance evaluation.

These unengaged employees are halfheartedly looking for another job, but feel that the next place may be just as bad as this one. They are basically checked out, and even their family feels their unhappiness and the weight of spending their workdays in a place they don't want to be, doing work they don't want to do.

Does this sound familiar? Is this a description of your employees? Or maybe even yourself?

If you picked up this book, you may already sense that this is a problem in your team, department, or organization. Maybe you even had an employee engagement survey that showed these results.

So, how can it be fixed? How can you change your unengaged employees into "rowers"—engaged, rowing toward the organization's mission?

You may not be able to rely on your company for help. Your organization may not understand the importance of engagement. Do you sense that you couldn't sell the changes needed to your "C" suite, or even to human resources? Maybe there is no budget for any initiatives to increase employee engagement.

The good news is that everything you are about to read in this book is something that you as a supervisor can do to increase engagement among each of your staff. Plus, *you can start today, and it won't cost a thing.*

Your best chance to make a difference is with the 50 percent of your people who are unengaged. If they can be turned on to be engaged and turned into "rowers," your organization can sail forward with increased productivity, better customer experience, increased safety, lower turnover, and increased profitability.

With the data showing that over two-thirds of an employee's engagement at work is directly due to their relationship with their supervisor, your employee's engagement score can be changed by things that you can do that will increase their happiness, fulfillment, and productivity at work.

Your HR department cannot raise your department's employee engagement score. They can only affect their own department's score. Each supervisor needs to engage their own employees. No set of mandates from the "C" suite, training programs, newsletters, employee appreciation events, or incentives will do it. You have to do it.

You are in a unique position to impact someone's life in a positive way, to make them a happier, more productive human being, and to affect their impact on their family.

What a gift!

Every interaction you have with your employees today influences their engagement.

ROGER'S STORY

Roger is an experienced paramedic working in an Emergency Medical Service (EMS) agency, responding to the city's 9-1-1 calls. His excellent clinical skills helped him gain a promotion to supervisor over a shift of paramedics.

Roger is young, but conscientious. He does an excellent job on the clinical side of supervising his staff, developing their patient skills. During his shift he supervises and assists with all trauma and cardiac patients, helping his young charges to sharpen their skills with CPR and handling traumatic injuries. He helps develop their customer service skills and handles patient complaints. Back at the station, he finishes up his shift with a review of the patient care reports from his staff and has the satisfaction of another successful shift with lives saved.

Meanwhile the mayor has directed city government departments to provide employee engagement survey results for a report he is preparing to highlight his accomplishments while in office. The EMS chief implements a survey to obtain the results for his agency.

Roger already struggles with engagement among his young staff. He had previously been their peer, but once he was promoted to their supervisor he had trouble separating the relationships. During emergency situations, the staff is a professional team working to save the life of the patient, but this changes between emergency calls when they engage in horseplay and do not file their reports on time.

Roger is also responsible for developing a "bench"—the next group ready for promotion—but he doesn't see any of his employees as mature enough to be a supervisor. When Roger gives his staff any negative feedback on their performance, he experiences pushback when they claim he is picking on them. As a result he avoids any uncomfortable conversations with the staff and just tries to concentrate on getting through each shift.

He doesn't trust his staff enough to delegate any new tasks or projects, so he takes on all new duties himself— he doesn't want to hear the complaints and would rather know it was done right by doing it himself. His turnover is high as his staff moves to other agencies that are offering sign-on bonuses, so Roger is spending a lot of his time onboarding and training new employees. As a result, he is overworked, stressed, and thinking about leaving his position and going back to school.

Roger's team is not engaged. Roger is probably not even engaged himself.

YOU KNOW IT WHEN YOU SEE IT

What is employee engagement, really? It's hard to quantify, but as Supreme Court Justice Potter Stewart famously said in 1964 about obscenity, "I know it when I see it."

An engaged employee stands out. They are committed to doing their jobs in the best way they can, and giving that extra effort to make sure they help move the organization's mission forward.

It's about intentions—the willingness to put in extra effort to help the organization succeed. It's about the emotional connection the employee has to the mission and the organization. They go above and beyond the requirements of their job. They enthusiastically strive to help the organization reach their goals, and they are happy and fulfilled at work.

Engaged employees are more productive, safer, happier, and less likely to leave their employer.

From this book, Roger will learn specific techniques that he can immediately put into use that will improve his staff's performance and his ability to manage them. He will understand how the steps he can take will affect their engagement.

He'll say, "My department was a nightmare and I read this book and got some tips for handling my team."

These techniques are great for new supervisors who are struggling with transitioning from a technical role to a leadership role. By learning how to engage their employees, they will also learn how to increase productivity and performance.

These techniques also work for all levels of managers, all the way up to the "C" suite. Although "C" suite employees tend to be more engaged by nature of their job, they still have a supervisor that accounts for 70 percent of their engagement score—the CEO.

Establishing a culture of engagement should be a business strategy, rather than a human resources department initiative. It should be a commitment from all leadership levels. But, if this is not the case in your organization, you can still use these techniques to engage your own employees.

These techniques can also be used in noncorporate environments, such as volunteer groups, homeowners' associations, and civic groups. Whenever people gather and form teams, the issue of team engagement exists.

FAKE IT UNTIL YOU MAKE IT

Leadership is your ability to hide your panic from others.

—LAO TUZ

How can you be the type of leader who engages your staff? Well, you picked up this book, so you are well on your way.

Leadership development programs often focus on trainings, theoretical information, and hypothetical scenarios. But that doesn't answer the question "What one thing could I do today to engage my staff?"

Even if you were just put into a supervisory position yesterday and have no idea what to do today, you can be a successful leader if you do one thing: learn everything you can about engaging each of your employees.

Leadership is a skill you can learn and practice.

Many leadership development programs are based on the idea of emotional intelligence (EI). The term was first coined in 1964 and gained popularity in 1995 through a book by the same name. It is based on the idea that the ability to understand empathy and the emotions of ourselves and others can lead to successful interpersonal interactions. In other words, if you can "read" your own emotions and control them, you can be more successful in relationships with others. And in your career.

Other words for emotional intelligence are "self-awareness" or the old-fashioned term: "maturity." EI means being aware of your emotions and not acting on them, treating others as you would like to be treated, apologizing, keeping your commitments, and accepting and learning from criticism. It also means being self-confident yet humble, empathetic, reliable, respectful, honest, positive, and supportive.

In other words, acting professionally.

So, acting maturely and professionally will help me be a good leader and engage my employees?

Yes, it's where you start. And, I'll let you in on a little secret I picked up during my thirty-plus years of business experience.

You can fake it until you make it.

You may not like a certain employee. You may feel frustrated. Your kids may have kept you up all night and you are dragging into the office. Whatever it is, you are now the boss and you can't show it to your employees. You need to appear calm and in control to be professional.

If acting professionally doesn't come naturally, sometimes we have to pretend!

You are creating an image. Look at the phrase "he acts professionally." See—it's an act.

This doesn't mean you are not being your authentic self. It means you are understanding that your behavior in the workplace is part of your work performance and may have to be different than the way you would act at home or around friends.

You can do it! Give an Oscar-worthy performance as a professional leader and get ready for the next steps to engage your employees.

KEY TAKEAWAYS

- Employee engagement is important to an organization's success because it positively affects productivity, turnover, and profitability.

- Engagement is about employees wanting to go above and beyond what is required.

- Most of an employee's individual engagement is due to their relationship with their direct supervisor.

- There are specific steps that supervisors can take, which will enhance their employees' engagement. The first is learning how to "act" professionally.

THE ENGAGEMENT RING

There are only three measurements that tell you nearly everything you need to know about your organization's overall performance: employee engagement, customer satisfaction, and cash flow.

—JACK WELCH

Now you understand the importance of employee engagement, how it impacts the bottom line of the organization, and how it will help your employees be happy and fulfilled at their jobs. You understand that you have a major role to play in their engagement. You've straightened up and are acting like the professional leader that you are meant to be.

What now?

Let's talk about the steps you are about to take in the following chapters and why and how they are going to engage your employees.

If you do an online search of "employee engagement survey questions," you get a variety of questions from a variety of sources. But, if you look closely at those questions, they usually boil down to asking the employee: How does your job make you feel?

Below is a sampling of "yes/no" survey questions that are commonly used and a description of what they are really asking about the feelings of the employee about working at that organization.

EMPLOYEE ENGAGEMENT SURVEY QUESTION	WHAT IT IS REALLY ASKING
My leaders keep me informed about what is happening.	Do you feel connected?
I have access to what I need to do my job well.	Do you feel supported?
I know what is expected of me.	Do you feel accountable?
I receive positive feedback when I do good work.	Do you feel recognized?
My manager shows a genuine interest in me.	Do you feel known?
My job provides me with a sense of meaning and purpose.	Do you feel important?
I feel stretched in a way that results in personal growth.	Do you feel challenged?
I feel like a strong member of the team.	Do you feel belonging?
I have a clear understanding of my career path.	Do you feel developed?
I can see how my work affects the overall success of the company.	Do you feel effective?
I always know what my goals and objectives are.	Do you feel measured?
I believe in my company's mission.	Do you feel committed?
My leader knows me as an individual.	Do you feel seen?
I am an important member of our team.	Do you feel trusted?
My team inspires me to do my best work.	Do you feel encouraged?
My manager demonstrates an interest in my well-being.	Do you feel valued?
My manager recognizes my full potential and capitalizes on my strengths.	Do you feel stimulated?
My leader encourages me to share and values my opinion.	Do you feel heard?
My supervisor helps me to succeed at work.	Do you feel respected?
I would recommend my company as a great place to work.	Do you feel proud?

There are twenty different "feelings" in the questions above, which can be sorted into four categories: relationships, included, needed, growing.

Helping supervisors to remember the elements of engaging their employees is the purpose of the acronym of the RING for The Engagement Ring. "R" is for the relationship with the employee's supervisor and colleagues. "I" is for feeling included, part of the team, in the loop, and belonging. "N" is for being needed, understanding how each job fits into and pushes the organization's mission forward, and "G" is for opportunities for personal and professional growth at work.

The feelings in the table above fall into the parts of the Engagement RING:

R	Relationships	seen, known, respected, encouraged, supported
I	Included	valued, heard, belonging, connected, trusted
N	Needed	important, proud, recognized, measured, committed
G	Growing	challenged, developed, stimulated, accountable, effective

ENGAGEMENT IN VOLUNTEER GROUPS

Engaged teams are often at work, but they can be in a volunteer group, on a board of directors, or in a homeowners' association. Anywhere there is a group that is led by one or more, there is the need for engagement of the members.

Richard was elected as president of the board for his neighborhood homeowners' association (HOA). The previous board had finished their two-year term with the goal of not angering any neighbors. If something was a "hot button" item, it was left to the incoming board. As a result, the new board had to deal with a property management company that was shirking their duties, condos that had been rented without proper approval, units that were not covered by insurance, asphalt in disrepair, and a new roof that leaked. To top it off, there were never enough in-person or proxy votes for a majority of the 160 units, so no new initiatives could be approved. HOA meetings were sparsely attended, residents didn't read the newsletters, and complaints and in-fighting among neighbors were rampant.

How could the Engagement Ring be used to get this group motivated to work as a cohesive unit?

If the HOA board understood what it took to get followers engaged, they could make a few changes using the elements of the Engagement Ring—relationships, included, needed, and growing.

For the "R" in the Engagement Ring, the board could start

with establishing relationships with the residents, such as having one-on-one meetings to see what their issues are and what direction they would like to see the association take. Then, the board could provide opportunities for the residents to develop relationships with each other—social activities, golf outings, and volunteer landscape clean-up days. The more friends they have in the association, the stronger their engagement will be.

For the "I" in the Engagement Ring, the individual residents need to feel included. Are they kept up to date on initiatives the board is considering? Do they feel they can run for the board and serve on the committees—or does it seem as if it is a clique running the HOA?

For the "N"—do the residents feel needed and are they proud of where they live? Volunteer opportunities should be provided and their efforts should be celebrated.

For the "G"—are there opportunities for personal growth in the neighborhood and in the association? Openings to serve on committees should be advertised and the activities offered should be stimulating. Committees should be held accountable and their efforts appreciated.

If Richard doesn't take steps to engage his residents, board, and committee members in his new role in the

HOA, he will not be able to move any initiatives forward and accomplish the goals of the organization.

In the next chapter, we will explore the most important element of the Engagement Ring—relationships.

KEY TAKEAWAYS

The elements of engaging your employees or members of your team form the Engagement Ring:

- Relationships—with their direct leader and their teammates

- Included—the feeling of belonging and being "in the loop"

- Needed—with a sense of purpose to their job and pride in the mission

- Growing—opportunities to grow personally and professionally

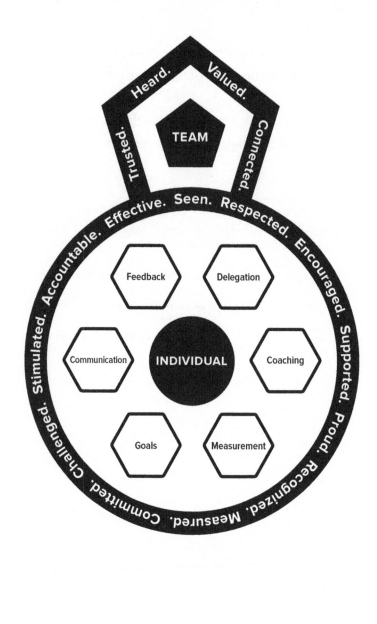

PART I

"R" IS FOR DEVELOPING RELATIONSHIPS

Personal relationships are the fertile soil from which all advancement, all success, all achievement in real life grows.

—BEN STEIN

R—RELATIONSHIPS (SEEN, KNOWN, RESPECTED, ENCOURAGED, SUPPORTED)

Engaged employees have strong relationships at work. The most important relationship is with their supervisor. They need to meet with their supervisor on a regular basis and share ideas, goals, and hopes. They need to feel their supervisor is their champion.

The number-one, most important thing you should take away from the topic of engaging your employees is that *your relationship is the most important factor in affecting their engagement.* As previously mentioned, the quality of their relationship with their direct supervisor makes up 70 percent of that employee's engagement at work.

You can now close this book and read no further. *If you do nothing else, do this: take steps to get to know your employees. Be in tune with their needs.* They want to be seen, known, respected, encouraged, and supported.

How do you do that?

Have regularly scheduled meetings where they know you "see" them and what they are working on, what their needs are, and what their goals are. Listen to them, be curious, and probe.

To paraphrase the poet Maya Angelou, our employees will forget what we said and what we did, but they won't forget how we made them feel.

The second part of the "R" of the Engagement Ring is that employees will be more engaged if they have relationships and friendships with their coworkers, colleagues, and teammates. Employees need to have a friend at work to be engaged. The more friends, the higher the engagement score.

Employee engagement is the responsibility of the supervisor, not the employee. So, how does a supervisor affect their staff's ability to make friends at work? You make an environment where friendships are sparked. Get everyone out of their cubicles. Have regular staff meetings, do icebreakers, do team-building activities. Assign small teams to take on projects or tasks.

Humans need a connection—they need relationships. They need to belong to a group, they need to feel that others accept them as they are, and they need to share inner thoughts with them.

We spend 36 percent of our waking hours with our "work" family. Those relationships matter. Without them, employees will seek other organizations to feel engaged. Or, even worse, they will stay with your organization and be one of the unengaged.

"R" IS FOR RELATIONSHIPS

- The most important relationship at work is between each employee and their supervisor.
- Meet with each employee on a regular basis to get to know them and their work more closely.

- Encourage friendships among the team.
- Employee engagement is the responsibility of the supervisor, not the employee.

CHAPTER 1

"DO I KNOW YOU?"

CONNECTING TO YOUR EMPLOYEES AS INDIVIDUALS

Everyone talks about building a relationship with your customer. I think you build one with your employees first.

—ANGELA AHRENDTS (SENIOR VICE PRESIDENT, APPLE)

In the story of Roger, he began to keep his staff at arm's length as he got pushback from them. Avoiding conflict became his way to get through his shift. He had no real connection with his employees now. The connection he had as their coworker was gone, and in its place was an awkward "no man's land" where Roger didn't know how to navigate. As a result, his employees were missing out on the chance to grow, to get ready for their turn at the role of supervisor.

They had a vague connection to the agency mission, knowing that they directly cared for patients and that the agency mission was about the care and treatment of the sick or injured in the community. But, they could just as well care for those sick and injured at another EMS service. So when there was a sign-on bonus offered at another agency, they jumped ship. With no other connection, they followed the money. As a result, turnover was high. This was costly to the agency and put undue burden on Roger and the other supervisors to continue to train new staff.

How could Roger turn this around? He wants to do a good job as a leader, but receives no real direction from his superiors. They also rose through the ranks based on their clinical skills and have tried to manage their staff as best they can, modeling their supervisory techniques on bosses they have had in the past—who may also have had no training in this area!

What to do?

The most important thing that Roger can do is use the Engagement Ring structure to manage his employees. By taking steps to engage them, he himself becomes a good leader.

The first step is to develop a relationship with his employees. This is the single most important thing. This one idea will transform his leadership ability.

RELATIONSHIPS THROUGH MEETING—SEE, I SEE YOU

The first part of the Engagement Ring is "R"—which stands for relationships. With statistics showing that over two-thirds of an individual employee's engagement score is directly attributable to their direct supervisor, this is the most important part of the Engagement Ring.

A culture of engagement can be passed down as a directive from the CEO, but it is the individual supervisor that is going to bring that to life. The first step is their relationship with each employee.

How well do you know your employees as individuals? Sure, you might stop by their desk on Monday morning to chat about the Sunday-night football game or ask about their kids, but how much time do you make for them in a structured way to find out about their work, their ideas, their challenges, wins, hopes, and dreams?

Letting the staff know your "door is always open" is not a substitute for a structured meeting schedule. A planned time to talk is important to establishing a relationship.

I like to call them "Check-In and Catch-Up" meetings or "See, I See You!"

A "Check-In and Catch-Up" meeting should take place once a week for thirty minutes. Since the acronym for "Check-In and Catch-Up" is CICU, if you say it out loud, it's "See, I see you," which really says it all. You want the employee to know they are seen and not invisible or irrelevant.

By putting a meeting on the calendar every week, you are signaling that the employee is important. It says that you, as their leader, felt they were important enough to hold a place for them in your busy schedule.

What should you talk about at these meetings? Everything related to their work and career. There should be a time schedule, an agenda, notes, and follow-up.

The agenda doesn't need to be written, but should be understood. It could be very loose. For a thirty-minute meeting, there could be fifteen minutes for the employee's issues and fifteen minutes for yours. The discussion should go over follow-up items from the week before, new projects, challenges, and obstacles. You can celebrate wins, talk about future professional growth—or the conversation may veer off into their family or personal interests from time to time. If the employee wants to talk about something, there is a reason—so stop and listen.

Did you know the same letters that make up the word "listen" also make up the word "silent"?

LISTEN—SILENT

You have to be silent to listen—and not be thinking about a rebuttal or what you are going to say next. Just hear them and think about what they are telling you. As you learn the coaching techniques in chapter 6, you can add these in to really learn about your staff member.

You will get a feel for how these meetings work as you go along—and for what your individual employees need from them. The main thing is to schedule them, hold them, make notes from them, and follow up on the items.

Although holding these meetings falls into the "Relationship" section of this book, they also serve other parts of the Engagement Ring—"I" for making the employee feel included, "N" because it gives you the opportunity to emphasize their part in the organization's mission, and "G" for a weekly opportunity to develop and grow your employee.

I once heard that a leader only has four things to do for their staff—set the direction, provide resources, remove obstacles, and develop their people. These are the topics that should be discussed at the CICU meetings.

Do they have what resources they need to do their job? What might their challenges to effective performance be? Where do they see themselves going in their career? You will also share with them information on where the department/organization is going and what their part is in it. This is where you will build trust and camaraderie.

Now, I can hear Roger and some of you saying, "How in the world am I going to fit in a thirty-minute meeting with each employee every week?!"

Here's how—in a forty-hour workweek, there are 2,400 minutes. If you spend thirty minutes on each employee, that is only 1.25 percent of your entire workweek per employee. Aren't each of your employees worth 1.25 percent of your time each week?

Plus, these meetings may take care of issues that would normally require an ad hoc meeting, so you may be actually saving time.

Roger may have a bit of a challenge because his employees are offsite for the entire shift, working in an ambulance. In addition, he and his staff are rotating on different shifts, so he doesn't supervise the same group each day he works. He will have to be creative in how he manages this, but it can be done.

If the end result is to make his employees feel seen, known, respected, encouraged, and supported—then Roger just needs to plug away on every shift, every chance he has, to make this happen. He knows who is on the schedule and can plan a week ahead how he can interact with that employee to find out what is on their mind, what their thoughts and dreams are, and how they are connecting with the organization and its mission.

Connecting with your employees is the most important thing you have to do every day. So find a way to do it.

In the book *The Mouse House*, author Pete Blank shared a story of going into his first supervisory experience with a difficult team. He tried everything to motivate them as a team and finally realized everyone is not motivated by the same things and started to meet with them individually. That's when he finally started to make a difference.

Managers need to be the strongest link in employee engagement. If they aren't, they will end up being the weak link and 70 percent of the engagement with that employee will be lost.

TRACKING THE RELATIONSHIP

Now that you are having regular meetings, it's time to be tracking your employees in written form. You should have a developmental file for each employee. This is just a file where you put information about the employee, weekly meeting notes, and documentation on performance issues. These are items that have not yet reached the level to involve human resources or to be put in the personnel file.

For your meeting notes, you can make up a form or buy a meeting agenda book with a section for notes and follow-up assignments.

In addition, you should have your employees listed on a spreadsheet where you are tracking things such as: where they are in the engagement rowboat, what steps you are taking to engage them, tasks or projects to delegate to them, goals, and measurements. Make notes on their personal interests. Some of these items we will discuss later in the book, but it's good to get started with employee developmental files and a spreadsheet where you can track everyone's progress.

A NOTE (AGAIN) ABOUT PROFESSIONAL MATURITY

In *The Truth About Employee Engagement*, author Patrick Lencioni says, "In order to be the kind of leader who demonstrates genuine interest in employees and who can help people discover the relevance of their work, a person must have a level of personal confidence and emotional vulnerability. Without it, managers will often feel uncomfortable, even embarrassed, about having such simple, behavioral conversations with their employees. They'll mistakenly feel like kindergarten teachers...even though their employees will be yearning for just such a conversation."

When you first start to have these meetings with your staff, it may feel awkward—especially if you, like Roger, are now supervising your coworkers. But again, "fake it until you make it." Have the conversations, "act" professionally, and it will get easier with each one.

In addition, help your staff get to know you. Maybe you could let them know about some of your quirks. Oh, come on—we all have them! What is it like to work for you? Are you cranky in the morning? Do you need to keep your door shut when you work on spreadsheets? Is your energy the highest in the afternoon? Tell them what makes you tick. You can avoid a lot of misunderstandings with your staff—and they will appreciate your honesty.

Leadership is a contact sport. Make contact on a regular, scheduled basis.

KEY TAKEAWAYS

- Have a prescheduled one-on-one meeting with your staff weekly to connect.

- Take notes at the meeting and follow-up.

- Find out what they need to do their job, their goals, and dreams.

- Have a spreadsheet and track your staff's progress in the Engagement Ring.

CHAPTER 2

"YOUR BFF AT WORK"

FOSTERING EMPLOYEES' RELATIONSHIPS WITH THEIR COWORKERS

There is nothing better than a friend, unless it is a friend with chocolate.

—LINDA GRAYSON

ENCOURAGING FRIENDSHIPS AMONG YOUR STAFF

Do you have a friend at work? Gallup has done a poll and found that if an employee has a friend at work, they are seven times more likely to be engaged at work.[2] The more friends, the more engagement.

---

2   Annamarie Mann, "Why We Need Best Friends at Work," Gallup, August 7, 2019, https://www. gallup.com/workplace/236213/why-need-best-friends-work.aspx.

We spend more time with our coworkers than our family, so it is logical that we would not enjoy the time at work as much if we didn't make connections with others.

Frances had a best friend in the customer service department where she worked. She and Deidre had lunch together. They started to socialize after work and eventually started taking trips together. When Deidre took a leave of absence to take care of her sick aunt out of state, Frances made the trip down one weekend for a visit. Eventually Deidre was not able to leave her aunt and return to work, and she resigned. Frances's engagement at worked slowly declined. She started missing deadlines and had problems with her accuracy. She was counseled repeatedly and eventually was put on a performance improvement plan. She did not improve and left before she was to be terminated. Hopefully Frances has found a new job with a new work friend.

A job needs to be more than a paycheck. Employees want to find organizations where they can form connections and relationships. But relationships can take on different forms, depending on how engaged the workforce is. For poorly engaged workers, having a friend at work may mean having someone to share gossip and complain about the boss with. But, for highly engaged workers, the friendship can further their engagement, resulting in innovation, productivity, and all the benefits that engagement brings.

So, friendship alone doesn't make for engagement. It is one part of the Engagement Ring.

How can you, as a leader, help staff have friends at work?

You can lay the foundation by making opportunities for your staff to get to know each other better.

First, hopefully you are already having regular staff meetings. If you aren't, these are important—not only to discuss work, department goals, and new initiatives—but they are equally important to get your staff in the same room on a regular basis and have group interaction.

Start each staff meeting with a short icebreaker. This puts everyone in the right frame of mind for group thought. An icebreaker results in laughter, and laughter builds teams. Team-building activities can be used to foster camaraderie and build group history. These are discussed more in chapter 4.

Offer opportunities for out-of-work experiences—retreats, off-site meetings, and volunteer projects. Make sure that the leaders promote and attend work-sponsored events.

Friendships are also built by shared experiences and stories—often an icebreaker or activity will result in a situation that is talked about fondly by group members in the future.

Several years ago, a leadership team I was on decided to get out of the office and do a paint class. It was one of those step-by-step classes and we painted the city skyline. That two-hour class resulted in years of connection among the group. First, we were amazed at the talent of a few of our members and saw them in a different light after that. Even those of us who did a basic job proudly displayed the paintings in our office. As we visited each other's offices, it was a tangible reminder of a connection we all had. The event was so memorable for the team that our CEO named the management group "Paint Club."

Although I have since left the organization, they continued to have an annual retreat. An afternoon out of the office doing a group activity pushes them out of their comfort zones and forces them to interact in different ways with each other. In the years since that first painting class, the group has done a Segway ride, an escape room puzzle, a tour of the city, and a scavenger hunt. All these activities gave them opportunities to continue to build friendships, but the group is still called "Paint Club" today.

ICEBREAKER IDEAS

Here are some icebreakers that can spur conversation. These are short and can be used at the beginning of a staff meeting:

- What was your first paying job?
- What did you want to be when you grew up?
- What is your latest binge on Netflix?
- What model was your first car?
- What is your favorite book?
- Tell two truths and one lie about yourself—and everyone has to guess which is the lie.
- Everyone writes down something the group members would be surprised to know about them. The leader reads the cards out loud, and the team needs to guess who said it.
- Divide into groups and find five things everyone in the group has in common.
- What was the first concert you ever went to?
- Name your favorite scary movie.
- Name the worst movie that you've ever seen.
- Name your favorite dinner.
- List three foods you'd prefer not to eat again.
- Name a city you'd most like to visit.
- If you're stranded on a desert island and have the option of bringing three items with you, what would they be?
- If you could be any animal, what would you be and why?
- If you could have any celebrity over for dinner, who would it be and why?
- What is your favorite ice cream flavor?
- What do you cook better than anyone else?

- What is your favorite candy bar?
- What would you want your last meal to be?
- What dish did your mom make better than any others?
- What is the weirdest thing in your purse or pocket and why do you carry it?
- If you could only vacation in one location for the rest of your life, where would it be and why?
- Have you ever won a trophy or medal, and what for?
- Would you prefer to travel forward in time, or back?
- List your favorite TV shows of all time.
- List your most disliked tasks to do around the house.
- What was your greatest accomplishment before the age of eighteen?

Have this list ready and pull out a question whenever you want to find out more about your staff, whether in a group or one-on-one. Everyone likes to talk about themselves, and these questions can be a fun and nonthreatening way to share.

THE PITFALLS OF SUPERVISORS BEING FRIENDS WITH EMPLOYEES

Roger had been friends with his coworkers before he was a supervisor. They were Facebook friends, texting non-stop, meeting up for drinks after the shift ended. They knew everything about each other's lives, both personal and professional. They enjoyed sharing the latest gossip they heard around the station and criticizing the decisions their bosses made.

But then, Roger was promoted and things changed. He couldn't share gossip that he was privy to in the leadership meetings. He now understood more about why certain decisions were being made. He was no longer "one of the crew."

Roger wanted to maintain the friendships, but found it was hard to do that outside of work and then act as a boss at work. How do you give negative feedback to your friends about their poor performance and then go out to the bar with them that evening? Roger struggled with his staff either disrespecting him, ignoring his directives, or giving him the cold shoulder when he held them accountable.

This goes back to being professional. You may have been promoted to supervise coworkers that are now your employees. You want to remain friends with them. How do you manage being both?

The answer is that you don't. *When you accepted that promotion, you made a commitment to being a part of the leadership team.* You can remain friends with your employees, but it is now a different friendship. You can't tell them things that are confidential within the leadership circle.

How to handle it? You need to let them know upfront how the job change is going to change the relationship. It's got to be an honest discussion about where you need to draw the line between friendship and work. Maintaining the friendship can be done, but it's going to take a lot of understanding, discretion, and professionalism on the part of both parties.

If it can't be maintained, you may need to decide which is more important to you—your career or your friend. And, if you have a friend that won't respect your new position and the line that you have to draw, then they may not be a true friend anyway. You may need to distance yourself from them. And, eventually the friendship may be lost.

This is tough for a lot of people, but here is where you decide which is more important. Those who are true friends will eventually understand. And, they will either settle into the new dynamic or move on to a new department or company. A professional leader maintains the course, not losing sight of the commitment he made in taking the promotion.

There also might be a person you supervise now that you didn't know before, but really hit it off with. Again, beware of developing this friendship beyond a cordial, professional relationship.

BEWARE OF SOCIAL MEDIA

Be aware of potential problems in connecting with your staff on social media. While a professionally oriented site like LinkedIn is an appropriate connection, personal sites such as Facebook and Instagram are a different story.

It's best to avoid connecting with your employees on social media sites. Not only would you have to be careful about what you post, but it could also pose a liability problem if you see your staff's posts about their health history, lifestyle choices, or religious or political views. The fact that you were able to see that information could come back later in a retaliation or discrimination suit, if they didn't like a disciplinary measure you were required to take and they falsely accused you of retaliating because of something you saw about them on Facebook.

The best step is to not accept or request connections to your staff on social media and, if you get promoted, to go through your social media lists and disconnect from your new staff.

They say it's "lonely at the top," and this is part of it. Although you also need a friend at work to feel engaged, as a leader you need to be more careful. Make friends with peers or with those outside your organization, and maintain your professionalism at work.

KEY TAKEAWAYS

- Create an environment to foster camaraderie among your staff.

- Give your staff opportunities to develop friendships.

- Icebreakers at the start of a staff meeting are a great way to encourage them to interact.

- Be aware of the pitfalls of developing or maintaining personal friendships with employees.

PART II

"I" IS FOR BEING INCLUDED

Coming together is a beginning. Keeping together is progress.
Working together is success.

—HENRY FORD

I—INCLUDED (VALUED, HEARD, BELONGING, CONNECTED, TRUSTED)

Engaged employees feel included at work. They are kept in the loop on communications about their organization and department. They are included in the big picture, beyond their daily job and tasks. They feel like an important part of their team.

Inclusion is a current buzzword, meaning that workplaces want diverse workforces—not just in the traditional sense with race and gender—but also in having employees with unique ideas, perspectives, and experiences they feel are important to the organization and who feel their ideas are valued.

The next step after hiring a diverse group of people is to make sure each one of them feels included, that they belong, and that their authentic self is valued. Those who feel they don't belong and are not a valued part of the team will not be as engaged or productive.

Feeling included is a fundamental human need. This is part of human DNA, a need from caveman days to form into groups as a means of protecting the tribe and accomplishing more than they could as individuals. The whole is greater than the sum of the parts.

Pat Wadors is chief HR officer at the LinkedIn company, and there is a video on YouTube that captured her speech called "The Power of Belonging." She talks about how LinkedIn has discovered how powerful it is to feel belonging at work. She describes inclusion as people feeling similar to their colleagues, yet feeling recognized for their distinct qualities. She calls this "DIBs"—diversity, inclusion, and belonging—and has found that it is the biggest driver of engagement at LinkedIn. This is so important that they have created a culture of "belonging" to enhance engagement. They encourage staff to help others feel they belong, give belonging moments, and tell belonging stories.

IN THE LOOP

Employees want to feel that they are important enough to know what is going on with their organization. Good news, bad news, any news. Too often, communications are tightly held within the leadership circle, with the feeling that lower-level employees either don't need to know, aren't interested, or can't be trusted with the information.

And to be fair, such information as new initiatives, possible budget cuts, and challenges from the marketplace don't come in as fully formed stories. By the time the upper-level employees in the "C" suite get the full picture on an initiative or challenge, the lower-level employees in the "Z" suite may already have made up their own stories about what is happening.

By maintaining transparency as much as possible, employees will feel included, empowered, and engaged. And guess what? *They may even have ideas on solving some of the challenges.*

What employees don't know, they will sense and then come up with their own scenarios.

Stay in front of the gossip and just tell them the truth, whenever possible.

"I" IS FOR INCLUDED
- Foster belonging
- Keep them in the loop
- Be transparent
- Manage the grapevine

CHAPTER 3

"LONGING FOR BELONGING"

FOSTERING INCLUSION IN YOUR TEAM

Belonging has always been a fundamental driver of humankind.

—BRIAN CHESKY

What is the opposite of inclusion?

Exclusion.

When you were a kid, were you ever picked last when dividing up teams? Have you ever come upon two friends whispering and laughing and they stopped when they saw you? Have you been the only kid in class not invited to a birthday party?

Each of us has felt the pain of being excluded.

It hurts. In fact, research has shown that this pain is as real as physical pain and affects the same pain centers. Being excluded is as real as a stubbed toe.

Marie was chief operating officer for a startup company. She reported to the CEO and became his sounding board. At first, she was his only employee. He rarely made a decision without Marie being involved, and she attended all meetings with him, from pitches to potential investors to signing the lease on their office space. As the company grew and the team expanded, Marie still enjoyed the feeling that she was a key member of the leadership team.

Then the CEO added a chief of staff position to the company. At first, Marie was glad to have another professional on board to help carry the load. But, things started to change. Marie was included in decision-making less often. Information was filtered through the chief of staff, who informed Marie, even though they both reported to the CEO. Meetings were frequently happening behind closed doors. Marie felt a loss of belonging and missed feeling like the important part of the team that she had enjoyed in the early years. She became less engaged at her job and eventually left that company, looking for another place where her skills were valued and she felt she belonged.

At work, if we are excluded from a meeting or decision-making process that we should have been in, it hurts. If we don't feel part of our work team, if they don't seem to value who we are and what we bring, it hurts.

And, pretty soon we stop being engaged. We stop giving that extra effort. We stop trying to integrate and adapt to the group.

Human beings are social. They need to connect with others—even the introverts among us. Being excluded socially is emotionally and physically painful.

THE IMPORTANCE OF BELONGING

In the 2018 Culture Amp study of over one hundred companies, they found that inclusion and belonging had the highest effect on employee engagement.[3] The study also reported, "People who feel they belong perform better, become more willing to challenge themselves, and are more resilient."

---

3   "Diversity, Inclusion and Intersectionality: 2018 Report," Culture Amp, accessed September 16, 2019, https://cdn2.hubspot.net/hubfs/516278/cultureamp-diversity-inclusion-2018.pdf.

In 1943, Abraham Maslow proposed a theory of psychology called the hierarchy of needs, which is widely used, even today. His theory is portrayed as a pyramid, with physiological needs such as shelter and food as the foundation at the bottom of the pyramid. The next level up is safety and security, followed by belonging and love. Self-esteem and self-actualization are at the top of the pyramid.

Maslow proposed that as each lower level of needs are met, the needs for the next level kick in. For instance, without food and shelter, humans aren't worried about their self-esteem. But, as soon as they have food and shelter, then there is the need for safety and security, followed by belongingness and love, followed by the rest of the pyramid. It's important to note that belongingness is in the middle of the pyramid and becomes a human need as soon as physical needs are taken care of.

BELONGING AND UNIQUENESS

Being included and belonging also have their complexities. The need to feel included is a drive to form lasting and positive relationships with their team. *People want to feel belonging, yet to feel unique at the same time.* This is a balancing act.

In their study of over 1,500 employees worldwide, Catalyst found that the more employees felt that they belonged to the team and the more they felt their own personal uniqueness was appreciated by the team, the more innovative they were and the more inclined they were to help other team members and to meet the group's objectives.[4]

FOSTERING A CULTURE OF BELONGING

How can leaders help employees feel they belong to the team? You, as the leader, must set the tone. A key motivator of belonging is spending time together. If you avoid some of your employees, the rest of the staff will pick up on that and not include them either. *They will take their cue from you.*

And, in reality, you may not like all your staff members. We don't all like everyone we work with. But each team member should be bringing something of value to the team, and you should appreciate them for that.

You don't need to invite them over for Thanksgiving dinner; just respect who they are and what they bring to the team.

What if this employee is not bringing anything of value

4   "Report: Inclusive Leadership: The View from Six Countries," Catalyst, accessed September 9, 2019, https://www.catalyst.org/research/inclusive-leadership-the-view-from-six-countries/.

to the team? Then that is a different issue, and you need to evaluate why you are keeping them on the team.

The leader and other members need to appreciate and emphasize the strengths of each of the team members. There are assessments that can be very helpful in having teammates understand each other's strengths and what each member uniquely contributes to the team. Assessment tools, such as the Myers-Briggs Type Indicator ®, DISC, and Profile XT, are a few that can be used to reveal characteristics for the group to understand each other.

A great way to make people feel they belong is to assign a mentor. The mentor could be from the leadership team or could be a peer mentor, on the same level as the employee. This connects them to the team on a one-to-one level.

Feelings of belonging are also fostered by making sure every team member has a voice. In staff meetings, don't let the loudest voices make the decisions. Find ways to draw out the opinions of the introverted members, such as having everyone put their ideas on sticky notes, pasted around the room. Or, use shared document folders online to get everyone's feedback on team projects.

Make sure decisions are made openly with the group, not behind closed doors with only a few team members. Provide a sense of connection, of common purpose, and of community.

Interacting with the team, valuing each member's opinions, and looking for opportunities to let team members work together and know each other better are all ways to foster a feeling of belonging.

What's the opposite of exclusion? Belonging, connected, valued, and included. And, you can make it happen for your team.

KEY TAKEAWAYS

- Humans have an innate need to belong to a group.

- They also need to be seen and appreciated for their individual strengths.

- Feeling excluded is painful.

- The leader should set the tone to make the employee feel they belong to the team.

CHAPTER 4

"THERE IS NO 'I' IN TEAM"

BUILDING YOUR TRIBE

The ratio of "We's" to "I's" is the best indicator of the development of the team.

—LEWIS B. ERGEN

Roger's crew doesn't really feel like a team. They are fragmented, both in physical proximity and in team spirit. They don't interact much at work due to spending their shift in an ambulance, running emergency calls. The only coworker they may see on a twelve-hour shift may be their partner. Much of their communication takes place on the radio with the dispatch center, which is the hub for all incoming 9-1-1 calls and ambulance dispatches.

Creating a strong team is an important part of a leader's responsibility. Staff that are stuck in their cubicles (or ambulances), working in silos, will not accomplish as much as a collaborative team. Those individuals may be completing the tasks and projects on their job descriptions, but they will be lacking the extra "oomph" of effort, innovation, and enthusiasm that being engaged brings.

Humans have an instinctive need to form into groups, teams, and clans. In the book *Tribal Leadership*, the authors wrote, "The success of a company depends on its tribes. The strength of its tribes is determined by the tribal culture, and a thriving corporate culture can only be established by an effective tribal leader."

THE THREE "C'S" OF TEAM BUILDING

To build a strong and engaged team, remember three "C's": communication, collaboration, community.

COMMUNICATION

Communication is important, not only with each individual employee, but also with the entire team. Team members need to feel they are "in the know" on communications.

Communicate, and then communicate again. Whatever you are sharing, share more and do it more frequently.

In *The Truth About Engagement*, Patrick Lencioni states, "When employees are engaged, they are emotionally connected to others and cognitively vigilant to the direction of the team...it's difficult to feel like you are part of a team when everybody has information that hasn't been shared with you yet or when team members don't fill each other in on what they are working on. Keep a level of transparency whenever possible with all members, even if the information doesn't directly pertain to every person on the team." This topic is also covered in the next chapter.

COLLABORATION

Collaboration is the act of working together, a joint effort to accomplish a goal. The leader can foster collaboration by assigning tasks and projects to groups, to form a temporary team. This is a great way to test out the team concept with your employees.

The teams may surprise you with innovative ideas and ways to accomplish goals. As they say, "Two heads are better than one."

Pair the team members up to complement each other's strengths and weaknesses. Share a scorecard on the progress of the team's goals.

Allow them to make mistakes. You will get more innovation and productivity from your team if they aren't afraid to fail.

COMMUNITY

Create a feeling of community among your staff. Use stories, have celebrations, share foods, have rituals, and share laughter to help the group bond.

Offer opportunities for interactions. You can start at the regular staff meetings (you are having those, right? If not, go back to chapter 2).

Start off with an icebreaker at the beginning of the meeting. The first few, you prepare—then assign team members to take turns to prepare and present one each month. There is also an extensive list in chapter 2.

Don't forget to celebrate! Have quarterly awards or recognition ceremonies, even if it just takes place at the staff meeting. Plan a group picnic at the end of a successful project or quarter.

BRAND YOUR TEAM

What is your team's dynamic, culture, and energy? In other words, *what's the vibe of your tribe?*

Figure out what it is, then capture it and brand it. Just as a product has a brand (think of Nike, Coca-Cola, and Starbucks), your team can have a brand.

Have a group discussion and brainstorm words that describe the team—or what they would like the team to be (remember, fake it until you make it). Post the words around the room, and have the group put them together into a brand statement for your department with the following: (1) establish who your customer is, (2) what you provide to the customer, and (3) why and how it ultimately affects the mission of the organization.

Here are some examples of departmental brand statements:

"The finance department prepares accurate, timely financial statements so that the senior staff can make quick decisions."

"The billing department provides support to our customers to turn around receivables in thirty days, so that the company has a cash flow to meet their goals."

"The IT department provides swift and friendly responses, repairs, and solutions to the hardware and software needs of the organization, so that our clients can be served without interruption."

Once the brand statement is set, have a contest for the team members to draw a logo and tagline or slogan. Create your own department's mission statement to align with the branding statement. Get shirts or coffee cups made with the slogan or logo to create a strong group identification.

TEAM CULTURE

Do you have your employees' backs? Are you ready to defend them? Your staff will be loyal if they know you are there for them. This also changes the group dynamic. If mistakes are not tolerated, it results in finger pointing, and that is the quickest way to destroy a team. Leaders should be their team's biggest advocate within the organization.

Do you have introverted team members? Be on the lookout for the team dynamic where the shyest members are not given an equal say. You, as the leader, must help develop and support the members that are reluctant to speak up. This establishes the team culture, and the other team members will follow your lead.

STORYTELLING

Steve Jobs said, "The most powerful person in the world is the storyteller."

A team is a tribe and should have a shared history. A history can be shared through stories. Storytelling is a great way to integrate a new member quickly and share information about the culture of a team. It can also motivate team members for new ideas—which then become a story for the future.

In *A Group Discussion Handbook: 15 Essential Questions (and Answers) That Ensure Successful Engagement*, author Thomas J. McCoy says team engagement can be fostered by stories, and leaders should "implement processes for collecting stories that can be shared with employees and the outside world."

How do you provide an environment rich for team building and stories? A great way is laughter. Provide opportunities for the group to work and laugh together. The team members need to know each other on a work level and personal level. They need to have opportunities to interact socially to become a cohesive team.

Find and encourage stories—inside jokes, happenings, and events—good or bad.

A structured team-building activity that can bring out stories is to have the group get together and have a few topics listed on the board such as, My First Day Working Here, My Favorite Story from a Business Trip, or My Worst Day at Work.

Go around the room and have everyone tell a story about one of the topics.

A WORD ABOUT HR TEAM-BUILDING ACTIVITIES

Your human resources department may have initiatives, such as employee picnics and holiday parties, to increase camaraderie among the staff. It is part of your job to attend those events. Now that you are a leader, it is your responsibility to support, promote, and be there for your organization and its activities. The staff has the choice to attend the company family picnic, but you don't.

Support the official team-building initiatives, but also develop your own within your department.

TEAM-BUILDING EVENTS AND ACTIVITIES

What are other ideas for bonding experiences? Here are some of my favorites:

IT'S PUZZLING

- Have a jigsaw puzzle set out on a table near the work area. Staff can stop to put a couple of pieces together to clear their minds for the next task. A team could sit down to talk out a challenge while adding pieces to the puzzle.

- Speaking of puzzles, have a team-building activity where you break into two teams and hand each team a bag of puzzles pieces to put together. The first team done wins. The trick is the groups soon realize that they only have half of a puzzle—and the other group has the other half. They have to then work together as a big group to finish the puzzle.

- Another puzzle idea. Give out puzzle pieces that are fairly large to each member at a staff meeting. They need to bring them back to the next staff meeting decorated—paint, fabric, glitter—however they each want to style them. Then have the group put the puzzle together. Frame and display, as it's a great piece of artwork!

- Another art idea. Hand out a small canvas (cheap to buy in multipacks at the craft store or online), brushes, and an assortment of paints. Cover your tables and have everyone paint a design of their choosing on their canvas. Let dry and hang together in the office as a mural.

GET-TOGETHERS

- Group ranking—without talking, have the group line up in order of one of the following: birth month, age, height, how long they have been with the company. You can do it as a competitive race with two teams— quickest and most accurate teams win. It makes the team members have to use nonverbal communication—and to see how well everyone knows each other!

- Do an office trivia game—develop questions to see how observant the group is with their surroundings. You could ask things such as, how many windows in the lobby? What color is the receptionist wearing today? How many people are in the finance department?
- Have a brown-bag lunch where you provide the drinks and dessert and play board games.
- Have a book club—maybe the company can purchase a variety of business books and small groups can read the same book and then report to the other groups.
- How about a volunteer day, working together outside the office for a charitable cause?
- Do you have access to a small room you could clear out to be a break room?
- Think of opportunities you can organize to get your team out of the office. How about a hiking staff meeting?

CHECK-IN WITH ROGER

How can Roger build his team? Paramedics arrive at work, check out the rig and the equipment, and hop on the vehicle. In a busy EMS system, there is not much downtime.

Roger's challenge is to connect the team to each other and develop some kind of team culture. This is much harder than if they were all together in an office each day.

By identifying what his employees' motivators are, Roger can come up with some ideas. He knows paramedics are motivated by patient care, clinical skills, and crew and patient safety. He also knows that meeting after the shift at a bar to relax and destress is where most of the bonding takes place. If Roger uses the three C's—communication, collaboration, and community—he can work in some of their interests and motivation.

Communication: Roger could do a weekly email to staff with the latest updates and tips for clinical care, safety initiatives, and news around the station. He could also include a weekly employee spotlight, with a photo and bio of a staff member, to let the staff get to know other team members.

Collaboration: During slow shifts, Roger could arrange to rotate crews to be brought in from the field for a short hands-on training or to form an employee committee to work on a project, such as proposing a uniform or equipment change.

Community: Building on the impromptu social events at the bar after shift, Roger could organize something more official after the shift at a bowling alley or pool hall where the crews could compete against each other and enhance camaraderie. Shared laughter and stories about staff members' pool or bowling skills become fodder for stories and team history.

These are some ideas for creating opportunities for team growth. You can find many more team-building ideas online. Find what works for the personalities and interests of your team members.

Be a strong tribal leader. Motivate, inspire, create new stories, and enhance the tribal culture, resulting in more "We's" than "I's" for the team.

KEY TAKEAWAYS

- Team building doesn't happen on its own—it must be created.

- Use the three C's to create teams—communication, collaboration, and community.

- Stories about the team become part of the history and culture of the team.

- You can set up activities to help create a history and stories and to motivate the team.

CHAPTER 5

"WE NEED TO TALK"

KEEPING EMPLOYEES IN THE LOOP

The single biggest problem in communication is the illusion that it has taken place.

—GEORGE BERNARD SHAW

Keeping communication flowing in an organization can be hard. Decisions are being made, new information is coming in, and there is constantly shifting perspective, ideas, and thoughts.

Zig Ziglar said, "Research indicates that workers have three prime needs: Interesting work, recognition for doing a good job, and being let in on things that are going on in the company."

THE COMMUNICATION LOOP

Terrell was scheduled for a flight with Airline A, going to the same city as Janet's flight on Airline B. Both flights were delayed due to weather at their destination. Airline B was immediately forthcoming with communications about the delay. Sharing the news over the loudspeaker with the waiting passengers, Airline B's gate agent announced as much as he knew about the weather delay. Airline A's loudspeaker was silent as the gate agents discussed the delay among themselves.

Janet was not happy about the delay, but went back to reading her magazine as she waited for additional information.

Terrell was not happy about the delay, and his anxiety increased as he saw the gate agents huddled together, not sharing any information. Terrell and the other passengers started surmising reasons for the delay and lack of information, fearing there were mechanical problems with the flight and discussing their fears around flying on a plane needing repairs.

Airline A's staff may have wanted to avoid sharing bad news, possibly hoping for the weather to improve without having to anger the passengers. But, without any information, Terrell and his fellow passengers imagined the worst.

Senior-level employees tend to be more engaged. They may have more autonomy, discretion in their work, and empowerment—but a big reason for higher engagement is that they are more "in the know."

Rumors about things that are happening—potential layoffs, mergers, or change of any kind—can scare employees. The lower the level of employee, the less they may know about what is happening.

As Winston Churchill said, "When the eagles are silent, the parrots begin to chatter." As with the airline passengers, when there is silence from the leaders, the followers will make their own assumptions.

HEAD OFF THE RUMOR MILL

How do you keep employees in the loop?

The team at a small marketing firm noticed a flurry of meetings behind closed doors with the owner and various visitors. Rumors started flying that the visitors were from a larger marketing agency in town. Staff started wondering if their firm was going to be bought out. When they asked the owner, she was vague in her responses. The employees started getting their resumes updated, in anticipation of their organization changing.

When there are changes happening, leaders need to be even more communicative than usual. Share what is happening—why, how, and when—as much as you can. Employees will be more likely to embrace the change, or at least accept it, if they were brought along on the journey.

What about when there is a real need for confidentiality? If something "leaked" out, would it jeopardize a deal, merger, or lawsuit? These are things that don't need to be told. The amount or depth of the communication should be appropriate to the situation and level of employee. But, if there is a part of it that can be shared—or even if you can acknowledge that there are things going on, but it's not the time to disclose details—employees will at least feel part of it.

Even if you tell them you don't know, they will appreciate that information. Be upfront with enough detail, but without causing fear or alarm.

SIMPLIFY THE MESSAGE

Communication should be provided in the context of what the staff can understand, explaining what it might mean for them, their department, and the organization.

Simplify. Be authentic in your communication style.

Don't give unnecessary details, but make sure the recipients understand the key takeaways.

Be aware of the effect of the new information to the staff. Listen to their questions and comments. Build trust and a sense of community. Be empathetic to their fears about change.

Share the thinking behind decisions, whenever possible.

Psychologist Jerome Bruner found that humans are twenty-two times more likely to remember a fact when it has been demonstrated by a story. Including stories can emphasize points and help the information stick.

Use the rule of threes—humans understand and remember three things at a time, which is the smallest number of things that make a pattern.

Be careful of nonverbal cues. If your words say one thing, but your facial expressions or tone of voice give another message, your recipients will believe the nonverbal information.

Whenever possible, obtain feedback from the team on the news. Ask for comments, ideas, and suggestions. If they feel that changes are happening to them, they may not be committed or accepting. If they feel they had a voice about the changes, they may accept it better.

Nobody thinks their own baby is ugly, so whenever possible let the staff have a say.

COMMUNICATION CHANNELS

How do you communicate?

Everyone has different learning and information processing styles. Using different communication channels, such as email, newsletters, staff meetings, town hall meetings, intranet, instant messages, and Slack channels, can be effective for different types of information.

If the information is time sensitive, an email or instant message might work best. If the information is better discussed in person to be able to answer questions, consider a staff or town hall meeting.

Scoreboards, dashboards, and other visual ways to communicate progress, meeting of goals, sales, and other achievements can also work. Tailor the mode of communication to the message and the audience.

Communication also needs to be an integral part of the weekly "See, I See You" meetings discussed in chapter

1. This is a perfect time to be able to give in-depth communication and answer any questions. Employees will feel even more engaged because they received the communications one-on-one, rather than in a staff meeting.

In our story of Roger, he felt he wasn't even in on enough information coming from his superiors to let the employees in on much. But he certainly knew about schedule changes, new clinical initiatives, and other things that would be of interest to the staff, and these are what he should be sharing.

You may not be privy to the entire big picture of communications, but share what you can to make employees feel "in the loop."

Things that the "C" suite doesn't want to share because they might frighten the "Z" suite would be better shared. Sometimes what the "parrots" may come up with when the "eagles are silent" is much worse than the truth. Employees will fill in the gaps of what they don't know. Just as Airline A's passengers imagined the worst.

So communicate, communicate, communicate!

KEY TAKEAWAYS

- Manage the communications, or the employees will make up their own version.

- Be as transparent as you can, but within confidentiality ranges.

- Keep "in the know" yourself.

- Be authentic and empathetic, and listen by being silent.

CHAPTER 6

"HEY COACH!"

DEVELOPING WINNING TEAMS

Management is about arranging and telling. Leadership is about nurturing and enhancing.

—TOM PETERS

COACHING YOUR TEAM

Coaching is quite a buzzword now. There are life coaches, health coaches, wellness coaches, training coaches, executive coaches, leadership coaches—the list goes on and on.

We all are familiar with a coach of a sports team, but what do all these other coaches do?

A coach helps to develop each team member's full potential.

A coach is a champion and cheerleader of their team members.

A coach provides encouragement and triggers awareness.

A coach helps their team learn, without teaching.

A coach assumes each team member wants to make the best choices.

A coach is not judgmental, only curious.

A coach believes each team member has the capacity to reach their goals.

You are the coach of your team. Is it a winning team? Are your team members ready to play, ready to win, ready to achieve the mission?

Why coach? Why not just tell your staff what to do to be successful and have them do it?

That's the old-school way. Tell, rather than ask, and solve their problems for them, rather than help them figure them out.

You know the old saying "You can give a man a fish and he'll eat for a day. Teach a man to fish and he'll eat for a lifetime." *Giving your staff the solution to a problem helps them for that day, but not for the long run.*

When an employee comes into your office with a problem for you to solve, they are bringing in a "monkey on their back." If you solve their problem for them, they have given you the monkey and you have taken care of it. But this doesn't prepare them for the next monkey.

Through some insightful coaching questions, you can help them get rid of the monkey without taking it on yourself. And, you are setting them up to avoid getting the monkey in the future by helping them figure out how the monkey got there.

NOT MY CIRCUS, NOT MY MONKEYS

Here are two excerpts from coaching sessions.

(Names have been changed to protect the innocent).

Paul: Hi, Boss!

Boss: Hi, Paul! What's on your mind?

Paul: Boss, I've got a monkey on my back, and I want to get it off my back and put it on your back.

Boss: Tell me about this monkey, Paul.

Paul: Well, he's a brown monkey, about twelve pounds.

Boss: How did he get on your back, Paul?

Paul: He climbed down from one of the trees in the parking lot as I came to work this morning.

Boss: What effect is he having on you by being on your back?

Paul: He's heavy and I am having trouble carrying him around.

Boss: What have you tried already to get him off your back?

Paul: Well, I gave him some bananas from the break room, but that just seemed to make him hang on tighter.

Boss: What advice would you give to a colleague that had a monkey on their back?

Paul: To see if their boss could help them get it off. That's why I came to you.

Boss: If I am hearing you correctly, you feel the only solution is for me to take the monkey?

Paul: Yes, that's right.

Boss: How would that make our department run more smoothly if the monkey were just passed back and forth?

Paul: Hmm, I didn't think about that. I guess I just was being selfish.

Boss: What are situations similar to this that you have handled outside of work?

Paul: Um, I don't know. I guess one time I found a neighbor's dog in my garage and it wouldn't leave.

Boss: How did you handle the dog, Paul?

Paul: I threw some treats out on the driveway, and when it ran out I closed the garage door real quick.

Boss: So what skills do you have that apply here?

Paul: I guess I could see if there is a way I could entice the monkey to leave on his own.

Boss: What's a small step you could take right now to gain some traction?

Paul: I could throw a banana to see if the monkey might chase it.

Boss: Given that there is never perfect information, if you had to make a decision now, what would you do?

Paul: I'll go back out into the parking lot and try it. Thanks, Boss!

Although that coaching session was a bit of fun, the lessons are real. Your employee may come to you with an interpersonal conflict, they may be stuck on a project, or they may want some guidance on their career.

Instead of solving it for them, take them through a series of questions to get to the heart of the matter and reveal what skills or experiences they have or have seen in the past that might be able to help them solve this current problem.

Here is a coaching session to help an employee develop some ideas for their future career path.

Boss: Thanks for meeting with me today, Paula.

Paula: Sure thing, Boss!

Boss: I wanted to talk to you about where your interest lies in your career and how I can help you grow.

Paula: Thanks, Boss! I hadn't really thought about that, though.

Boss: Since you started your career with us, what positions have you been in?

Paula: Well, I started selling popcorn under the bigtop, and now I have moved up to ticket sales at the front window.

Boss: How have you liked those positions?

Paula: I like them well enough.

Boss: What has been your favorite parts?

Paula: I guess I enjoyed selling the popcorn because I was in the midst of the circus.

Boss: So what do you like most about being in the circus atmosphere?

Paula: I love the clowns.

Boss: What is it you like about clowns?

Paula: I like that they can make people laugh.

Boss: Tell me about making people laugh.

Paula: You make people happy, and it's something I would like to do.

Boss: Is your interest in making people laugh or in being a clown?

Paula: It's a dream I have always had to be a clown. But, I would never be able to do it.

Boss: What would keep you from being able to do it?

Paula: I wouldn't know how to get started.

Boss: What steps have you seen the other clowns take to get started?

Paula: I know the clown Clement, and he went to clown school.

Boss: How could you model what Clement did to move you closer to your dream?

Paula: I guess I could apply to clown school. Would you write me a letter of recommendation?

Boss: Of course, Paula.

THE COACHING MINDSET

Coaching is listening, questioning, probing—not solving. That's when the real learning happens, when they figured it out for themselves.

A question can reveal a blind spot. Ask powerful questions to draw out what they already know, but don't know they know.

Don't give advice, but let them come to their own answers. It's consulting, not coaching, if you give them a solution to their problem.

Coaching takes patience and practice. It won't come naturally at first.

It starts with listening. Really listening. Listening out of curiosity, beyond what their words are saying.

In his book *The Way to Coach*, author Andrew Neitlich says, "The art of coaching is largely about developing the capacity to listen."

Be silent. As mentioned in chapter 1, LISTEN and SILENT have the same letters. Get comfortable with silence. Let it work for you. Silence allows the listener to think their own thoughts without listening for what you are about to say. Sometimes the best aha moments happen in silence.

Ask questions to move their thought processes along. Avoid "yes" or "no" questions, as they don't reveal anything. Also, avoid "why" questions, as they may sound like a judgment.

Notice their body language and energy as you "peel back the layers of the onion" with follow-up questions.

Reflect back what you heard. The act of them listening to their own words out loud and listening to you repeating back what you heard can reveal a blind spot or cause a "lightbulb" moment.

In *The Coaching Habit*, author Michael Bungay Stonier says the "seemingly simple behavior of giving a little less advice and asking a few more questions is surprisingly difficult...when you're asking questions...the conversation can feel slower and you might feel like you've somewhat lost control of the conversation (and indeed you have. That's called 'empowering')."

Coaching does not need to be time consuming. It's called "laser coaching," where you take fifteen minutes or less to coach someone through a specific problem. The coaching sessions above with Paul and Paula were short, but effective.

Coaching can be done daily with your staff. Whenever you see an opportunity to help them look at a problem in a new way, to reframe their viewpoint about an issue, or to develop a plan for moving forward, it's an opportunity to coach.

Coaching increases your staff's autonomy and mastery, freeing you from having to jump in and fix their problems.

Coach your way to a winning team!

KEY TAKEAWAYS

- Coach your team to develop skills to solve their own problems.

- Coaching requires patience, practice, and listening skills.

- Use listening and silence to coach effectively.

- A coaching habit is not time consuming and can be done daily.

PART III

"N" IS FOR BEING NEEDED

All employees have an innate desire to contribute to something bigger than themselves.

—JAG RANDHAWA

N—NEEDED (IMPORTANT, PROUD, RECOGNIZED, MEASURED, COMMITTED)

Engaged employees feel needed at work. They know how their job duties fit into the organization's mission. They feel their work is important. They know they are doing well and feel they have a mastery of their job.

Roger's paramedics felt connected to the clinical mission they had trained for, which was the health and well-being of their patients. However, they could fulfill this mission at any EMS agency. Roger's challenge was to connect these paramedics to the mission of his organization, to make them feel committed and engaged there.

How could Roger's organization differentiate themselves from any number of EMS agencies in their area?

Through culture.

Workplace culture is defined as the "personality" of the organization. It's a shortcut to what is valued, promoted, and believed. It's a series of actions that demonstrate what is important to the company.

Workplace culture is built day by day, interaction by interaction.

A workplace culture that is proud of its mission and promotes it clearly is appealing to employees. They know what they are working toward and are proud to work for such a company. If they clearly understand how their day-to-day tasks move the mission forward, they feel even more connected.

A workplace culture that holds employees accountable to successfully achieve those daily tasks and provides measurement techniques that let the employees know how they are doing is even more likely to have an engaged, productive, and fulfilled team.

A workplace culture that welcomes new staff and clearly communicates the mission and culture right away is more likely to create engagement. This connection can be strengthened with "stay interviews," regular meetings to obtain feedback about each employee's experience working there.

And a workplace culture that extends a warm send-off and maintains connections with former employees will be rewarded with loyal advocates who will sing the company's praises out in the world—and may even return to work there.

When employees feel needed, connected, and important, the organization will benefit.

"N" IS FOR BEING NEEDED

- Connect them to the mission.
- Have a solid onboarding process.
- Do semiannual stay interviews.
- Let staff leave on good terms.

CHAPTER 7

"JOB GPS"

CONNECTING THE EMPLOYEE TO THE MISSION

If you don't know where you are going, you'll end up someplace else.

—YOGI BERRA

THE STORY OF GAIL AND STUART

Gail is a server at a busy diner, frequented by truckers. She consistently makes 25 to 30 percent tips on her customer's checks. Her manager values Gail as an employee. Not only is she productive, friendly, and helpful, but she turns over her tables 10 percent faster than her coworkers and her customers on average spend 25 percent more per check than any other server, because she enthusiastically promotes the diner's array of homemade desserts. Gail is an engaged employee.

Stuart is a server at a high-end steak house in the same town as Gail. His average tip per check is 18 percent. His manager feels Stuart is a lackluster employee. He sometimes needs to be reminded to return from his break on time, and there have been a few customer complaints about his service. Stuart seldom remembers to ask his tables if they would like appetizers or dessert, so his average customer spend is the lowest per server, as is his table turnaround time because he is slow to bring the customer's check at the end of the meal. Stuart is an unengaged employee.

The mission, vision, and values of both restaurants have to do with customer service and profitability. Assuming that their position descriptions are probably very similar also, which of these employees has embraced the mission of their organization? It's easy to tell it is Gail, without even observing her work, based on the metrics used to track servers' performance.

Knowing how their daily work directly affects the mission of the organization is a key factor in employee engagement. And following that up with a measurement system that the employee can see daily further increases their connection.

Both Gail and Stuart knew how they were doing at work based on the metrics of tips, average spend per check, and table turnaround time. For Gail, it was probably a motivator and made her even more engaged. For Stuart, it may be that his heart is not in being a server and he needs to find another line of employment.

MISSION IMPOSSIBLE

Do you know your organization's mission? Could you say it right now? Can you tell a story about it to make it stick in people's imaginations?

If you, as a leader, cannot say "yes" to those questions, how can your staff know how their job, projects, and tasks relate to the mission? And if they don't feel they make a difference in the mission, they may feel their job—and they—are not needed.

"Connect the dots between individual roles and the goals of the organization. When people see that connection, they get a lot of energy out of the work. They feel the importance, dignity and meaning in their job," say Ken Blanchard and Scott Blanchard in *Do Your People Really Know What You Expect From Them?*

Gallup data show that only 40 percent of millennials feel strongly connected to their organization's mission and that only 34 percent report that they have a heard a story in the past thirty days about how their company impacted a customer.[5] Not hearing these customer stories could be one reason why millennials feel disconnected at work. Stories help bring the mission to life.

Those who work directly with your customers will likely feel the mission more keenly than a clerk tucked away in the billing department. Especially if you are in charge of a support department, you will need to bring stories back to your team about how the organization impacts its customers and its mission, since they may have limited direct interaction with the customers.

How connected do you feel to your company mission? How does your organization contribute to society? To the community in which it is located? To the world, the planet? *The employees should be proud to support the mission, proud to be employed there.*

Here are some well-known company mission statements:

Uber—"We ignite opportunity by setting the world in motion."

---

5   Brandon Rigoni and Bailey Nelson, "Millennials Not Connecting with Their Company's Mission," Gallup, August 7, 2019, https://www.gallup.com/workplace/236342/millennials-not-connecting-company-mission.aspx.

Tesla—"To accelerate the world's transition to sustainable energy."

Starbucks—"To inspire and nurture the human spirit—one person, one cup, and one neighborhood at a time."

Is your company's mission statement as succinct and compelling as these examples? Most companies' are not. It may take some creativity to bring the average mission statement to life.

CONNECTING THE DOTS

In his book, *Employee Engagement: Lessons from the Mouse House!* Pete Blank explains the Disney philosophy as the concept of "big picture to small parts," knowing what your part of the larger mission is. "Cast members who worked in the kitchens of quick-service restaurants were not just cooking burgers. They believed a family was going to come to their theme park and their restaurant, and that family was going to order four of their cheeseburgers, and that family was going to enjoy that meal as part of their Disney vacation. Training every cast member to know how important their role was to the entire show created more-committed employees."

How well does your staff know their position description, not to mention the agency mission?

Sit down with your employees to go over their written job description. (Don't have one? Time to write one!). Find out if they think it is up to date and accurately reflects the duties they are responsible for. If not, it's time to update it. Either the employee is doing duties that are not part of their job, or the job description is outdated.

Now compare the organization's mission and the employee's job description. Go over each with the employee, working together to gain an understanding of how they fit together.

They don't fit together? If the job description accurately reflects the duties in that job, then maybe that job is not needed. Every position should be a cog in the wheel that moves the mission. Any other job is just fluff.

There also should be departmental goals based on the organization's mission. These are what your department needs to achieve to be successful and do its part to move the mission forward. Make sure the team understands these and how their own job goals fit in.

Communicate these goals, track progress—and repeat. This topic should be discussed often and thoroughly, reminding the team what their purpose is.

MISSION ACCOMPLISHED THROUGH MEASUREMENT

In *The Truth About Engagement*, Patrick Lencioni states that the three root causes of job misery are "anonymity, irrelevance, and immeasurement," and that the antidotes to these miseries are to make sure the employee knows who their work impacts, how it impacts them, and how to assess their own progress or success. "Whatever measurement is used, it's important that they be able to monitor their own success and that when they leave their shift, [they] know how they performed that day. Employees who can measure their own progress or contribution are going to develop a greater sense of personal responsibility and engagement than those who cannot." Lencioni surmises that is why so many salespeople are engaged at their job, because sales and commissions are their measurement.

Just as an athlete knows their score at the end of the game, employees should be able to know how they performed at work at the end of their day.

Once the employee understands their goals, they need to know if they are meeting those goals. You have measurement tools that you are probably already using to measure the success of your department. There may be dashboards, time tracking, quality, and quantity output measures. How could these be used to measure the employee's work and help them know their progress on a daily basis?

Remember our restaurant servers, Gail and Stuart? They know every day how many tips they receive, how fast they turned over their tables, and their average spend per customer. Our salesperson knows how many sales they made each day. The basketball player knows how many points she scored each game.

Our friend Roger already tracks the time his staff spends on each call, how quickly they turn over the patient at the hospital, and how many cardiac-arrest saves they have on each shift. These could be communicated to each employee as they get off their shift or at the end of the week.

How about the finance department? They could track how many bills were paid on discounted terms, how many invoices were sent out per day, and how many days it took to close the books for the month.

How about building maintenance? They can track how many work orders are completed in a day, how long it takes to clean the building, and how they are managing a preventative maintenance schedule.

Help each employee figure out what to track to see how

well they are performing on a daily or weekly basis. Everyone should know if they are making a difference and if they are moving toward the mission. Just like Gail and Stuart.

KEY TAKEAWAYS

- Bring the mission to life in your employees' eyes with stories, acronyms, or shortened versions, so that they can connect to it.

- Use the organization's mission and each employee's position description and work out the connection.

- Create goals with the employees that connect their daily tasks to their role in the mission.

- Work with the employees to create daily goals that they can measure themselves to immediately know how they are performing.

CHAPTER 8

"I'VE GOT YOU, COMING AND GOING"

ONBOARDING, STAY INTERVIEWS, AND BOOMERANG EMPLOYEES

Train people well enough so they can leave. Treat them well enough so they don't want to.

—RICHARD BRANSON

Sue arrived to work on her first day. Although she had worked for the company six years prior, she had gone on maternity leave and not returned. Now she was rehired.

Sue is an example of a "boomerang" employee. She had

been a valued employee and was treated well by the company. When she resigned after her maternity leave, she was wished well, congratulated on her new life, and told to keep in touch. As a result, she had a good feeling about the company, which led her to reapply when her child started school. The company gained back an experienced employee.

During the years that Sue was gone, she spoke well of the company and their culture and promoted it to friends as a great place to work. As a result, the company recruited some new employees and customers.

Unfortunately, on her first day back, no one welcomed Sue. Her new supervisor was offsite that day. He had forgotten to alert the IT department, and Sue's computer was not set up. When he was finally located by phone, his directives were vague and Sue spent the first day reading the employee manual. It was two days later before HR gave her any paperwork to fill out, or her boss gave her clear directions. In six years many things had changed, yet the company thought she didn't need any formal orientation or onboarding process.

It made Sue feel that her hire was an afterthought. She is still with that company fifteen years later, but has never forgotten the lack of welcome and how she felt that day. She is now their HR director and has made sure that no one else experiences a first day like that.

When I was hired for my first director-level job, it was a big jump in level, responsibility, and authority. The company was new to me, and I am sure I looked like a deer in the headlights as I walked in my first day. I remember trying to maintain my composure and act confident, but was nervous about the new job and making a good impression. I was even getting an office for the first time in my career, rather than a cubicle.

When I was shown my office, I nervously opened the door to find a bouquet on my desk, with the flowers made from candy bars. The card attached was signed by my new boss, and he said he wanted to welcome me that day, but he had to be out of the office. He also noted that his administrative assistant had made the bouquet. I walked over to thank her, and she handed me a letter from my new boss. In it, he gave me an overview of my responsibilities, an organizational chart, and what my first challenges would be. He ended by saying how thrilled he was to have me on board and excited about what I could bring to the team.

I still have that letter and use it as the standard for making my employees feel welcome. That welcome set the tone for my employment, and it felt like it kick-started my career there.

How did my first day go, as opposed to Sue's? Eventually we both settled in to the jobs and did well at the companies. But, neither of us forgot the experience of our first day.

ONBOARDING

Onboarding is the process of welcoming and integrating new employees into the workplace. As you can see from the examples above, proper onboarding—or the lack of it—sets the tone for employment and becomes part of the workplace culture.

Do you remember your first day of work? Most people do. It's like the first day at a new school. And it feels like you are right back to being a kid again.

Gallup analytics found only 12 percent of employees, including leaders, think their company does a good job of onboarding a new employee.[6] These companies are missing out on the opportunity to lay the foundation for the employees' engagement and productivity.

Hopefully your organization has a formal onboarding or orientation program, but that doesn't relieve you as the supervisor for creating your own welcoming process. Remembering your first day at your company, what would have made you feel welcome? What information did you

---

6   "Why the Onboarding Experience Is Key for Retention," Gallup, August 19, 2019, https://www.gallup.com/workplace/235121/why-onboarding-experience-key-retention.aspx.

need to know? How could you have felt part of the team right away?

A welcome letter is a great way to get started. It can be sent before the first day of work. Let the new hire know you are excited to have them, you were impressed by their interview, and you feel they will make a great member of your team. A small gift, plant, or candy on their desk with a handwritten welcome note to greet them on their first day will make a lasting impression. Even some company trinkets can make new staff feel part of the team.

Here are some ideas for onboarding a new employee within your department:

- Send a welcome email before their first day.
- Provide an organizational chart of the department and names of each team member.
- Have their badge ready.
- Have their computer and access set up.
- Assign a buddy or mentor to give them a tour and take them out to lunch.
- Go over their position description and the company mission to show the connection.

Build the Engagement Ring for new employees as soon as possible. Individual meetings with their supervisor and teammates will make them feel included. Provide lots of communication, make them feel needed, and connect them to the mission as soon as you can.

Spend some time planning your onboarding process and defining the culture or "personality" of your department. How do you communicate a "shortcut" to what is valued there? Don't wait to have the new employees figure it out. Tell them what you are about.

STAY INTERVIEWS

You do interviews to hire an employee and exit interviews when they leave. Through those interviews, you know why a new employee wants to work for your organization and why an employee leaves your employment.

But what about the employees who don't leave? Do you know why they are staying? If not, find out through a stay interview.

A stay interview is done separately from a weekly one-on-one meeting and separately from their annual performance evaluation. It is a special meeting done at least once a year (and maybe twice a year for the first year of employment) to find out what employees like and don't like about their job, you as their supervisor, and their company.

Here are some questions to ask:

- What are your career goals?
- What do you like about working here?
- What could be improved about the workplace?
- What skills would you like to build?
- What would help you do your job better?
- Have you thought about leaving?
- What makes you stay?
- What would you like to be doing one year from now?
- What's one thing I could do to make your employee experience better?

Find out what your employees' goals are and how you can help them reach them. What obstacles are they facing and what resources do they need? What does the organization do well for their employees? What could be better?

Here is a caveat. If you do not have a culture of openness, honesty, and accepting feedback, don't bother doing stay interviews. If you will not take action based on the feedback, or even worse, will resent the employee's honesty, the stay interview will do more harm than good.

But, if you are open to finding out the truth, no matter how harsh, then you will get a lot of good information for recruiting, hiring, and retaining employees for the future. As an added bonus, *the employees will feel seen, heard, and that their opinion mattered.*

BOOMERANG EMPLOYEES

In the book of the same name, *The Boomerang Principle*, author Lee Caraher defines the principle as "the belief that organizations that allow and encourage former employees to return have a strategic advantage over those that don't." She doesn't believe it is disloyal for an employee to leave, saying, "The most loyal act an employee can do is leave when he is no longer...engaged, productive, or happy."

Have you ever known someone who, when crossed, cuts the person off from their life? Some workplaces have a similar culture—if you leave, you are disloyal, so you are "dead" to them. Former employees are not welcomed back for a visit. Once gone, stay away. Out of sight, out of mind.

According to the Society for Human Resource Management (SHRM), the average U.S. turnover rate is 18 percent.[7] That means that 18 out of every 100 employees will leave employment this year. Hopefully if you use the techniques in this book and engage your employees, you could reduce that rate at your organization. But realistically, you will still lose a certain percentage of employees, no matter how engaged your workforce.

---

7   "2017 Human Capital Benchmarking Report," SHRM, December 2017, https://www.shrm.org/ hr-today/trends-and-forecasting/research-and-surveys/Documents/2017-Human-Capital-Benchmarking.pdf.

The companies that cut ties with former employees are losing out on a valuable chance to have a loyal champion. Employees who leave to escape a toxic environment will not be a champion. But those who leave a good company, with good feelings—and who just want to strike out for new horizons—have the potential to communicate to their network about your organization as a great place to work and a great place to be a customer. They will send recruits, customers—and may become a customer themselves. And someday they may come back to work for you—with an expanded skillset and experience that you did not have to pay for.

Keep former employees on your mailing list, invite them back for visits, and treat them as a college treats their alumni. You have nothing to lose and everything to gain.

Nurture your staff from their first day of work to their last.

KEY TAKEAWAYS

- Integrate each new employee into the organization with an onboarding process within your department.

- Make stay interviews part of your process to obtain positive and negative feedback about the employees' experience at your company and within your department.

- Be open to honest feedback obtained at the stay interviews, and be prepared to act on it.

- Keep a connection with all employees who leave, encouraging a relationship so they remain a champion of your organization.

PART IV

"G" IS FOR GROWING PERSONALLY AND PROFESSIONALLY

The growth and development of people is the highest calling of leadership.

—HARVEY S. FIRESTONE

G—GROWING (CHALLENGED, DEVELOPED, STIMULATED, ACCOUNTABLE, EFFECTIVE)

Engaged employees feel there are opportunities for personal and professional growth at work. An effective leader will encourage, foster, and offer opportunities to stretch and develop their staff.

Sometimes development may seem negative. Difficult conversations and critical feedback can be uncomfortable for the supervisor and painful for the employee. But these conversations can adjust the direction for the staff member and set them on the right path.

Other development is positive. This includes giving complimentary feedback and delegating more complex tasks to staff to stretch them and prepare them for future promotions and more responsibility.

How could our buddy Roger develop his staff of paramedics? First, he needs to find out what their aspirations are. Then he needs to be their champion and advocate within the organization and find resources to help them move toward their goals.

It's your job to encourage your employees' personal and professional growth.

Leadership is about unleashing the team's full potential. As Jack Welch said, "Before you become a leader, success is all about growing yourself. After you become a leader, success is about growing others."

So, get set to grow your staff.

"G" IS FOR OPPORTUNITIES FOR PERSONAL AND PROFESSIONAL GROWTH

- Don't shy away from direct conversations that need to happen
- Give consistent positive and negative feedback, as needed
- Find stretch assignments to delegate and grow staff
- Provide and encourage developmental activities on a regular basis

CHAPTER 9

"SAY WHAT?!"

HAVING DIFFICULT CONVERSATIONS IN THE WORKPLACE

10 percent of conflict is due to difference of opinion and 90 percent is due to delivery and tone of voice.

—UNKNOWN

CONFLICT AND CONFRONTATION

When it's time to talk to an employee about an uncomfortable situation, corrective action, discipline, or anything unpleasant, it can fill you with dread.

Shanna managed a car wash and had an employee, named Chris, who developed a body-odor problem. Vehicles cleaned by Chris needed to be aired out before customers could claim their cars. Otherwise, Chris was a great worker.

For the first few months after being hired, this had not been a problem, but Chris's girlfriend broke up with him and his hygiene took a hit. With employees and customers complaining, Shanna needed to address the situation. Feelings of sympathy about his personal problems couldn't get in the way, as this issue was disrupting business. But Shanna was dreading the conversation.

How do you have a conversation like this?

SAS IT!

S—See the situation from the other person's side
A—Assume they want to do the right thing
S—Script the conversation

In his book *Difficult Conversations: How to Discuss What Matters Most,* author Douglas Stone says, "Difficult conversations are almost never about getting the facts right. They are about conflicting perceptions, interpretations, and values."

Getting into the mindset of the other person and acknowledging that they probably don't mean to be causing this issue is the first step. Most people have positive intent.

Certainly at work, with their livelihood at stake, most employees want to do the right thing.

LOOK AT IT FROM THEIR PERSPECTIVE

Prepare what you are going to say. Write it out as a script. Try to anticipate how they will respond. If necessary, practice on someone else and role-play the conversation.

This conversation should be in person. Email can be tempting to avoid the uncomfortable face-to-face interaction, but written communication can easily be misunderstood because your recipient cannot see your body language, tone of voice, and facial expressions.

Meet in person, maintain eye contact, and let them sense your compassion.

During the conversation with Chris, Shanna should take a neutral tone and simply lay it out in the following manner: describe the issue, describe the impact, request the expected change of behavior, and end with a positive statement for the future.

She could say, "It has been noted that you have a body odor and are leaving a smell behind in the vehicles you are cleaning. This has caused complaints from customers and other employees. Please correct this hygiene problem before you come to work tomorrow. I value you as an employee and know you can get back to the way you were when you first came here."

It's not the supervisor's role to offer the how or why. Although Chris may make excuses (shower is broken, already wears deodorant, no one else in his life complains about it, girlfriend broke up with him), whatever it might be—and however sad—the only conversation needs to be a description of the issue, acknowledgment of how it is impacting the business, the specific change of behavior required, and reaffirming the relationship and belief in the person.

Make sure you have these conversations about something that is objective, based on measurable facts, rather than subjective—which is based on personal feelings, opinions, and emotions. For instance, saying that someone has an attitude problem is subjective, but describing a loud tone of voice, assertive body language, and strong language is objective.

It has been said that the rule of thumb is that if it is something that could be seen on a videotape, it is objective. Although, with the case of Shanna's stinky employee, video wouldn't capture it. Unless it had "smell-o-vision."

When appropriate, be sure to follow up on the conversation. Shanna should meet with Chris the next day to see how he is feeling about the conversation, which also will allow her to get a "sense" about if he has made the hygiene changes necessary.

All conversations with employees that could eventually result in corrective action should be documented in writing afterward. Although Shanna's conversation with Chris will hopefully spur him to make the necessary changes, she should still document the date, time, and discussion in case the behavior continues in the future. If the behavior becomes a pattern, Shanna will have a paper trail of the counseling sessions, and HR will thank her.

THE ROLE OF ANGER IN THE WORKPLACE

Sometimes having difficult conversations can result in anger on the part of the employee, or even the supervisor. The employee's reaction may cause a reaction in the supervisor.

What is the role of anger in the workplace?

There is no role for anger in the workplace.

Anger is an emotion that is okay to feel, but not to act on at work (or possibly anywhere!). But, especially as the boss, you have an obligation to maintain a professional demeanor.

Your buttons might be pushed. The employee may react by verbally attacking you personally to get a reaction. You are a human being, too. So, be prepared to end the meeting, if necessary.

Supervisors should prepare a script for those times when an employee demonstrates anger, or if they themselves starts to feel the emotion. The solution is to remove yourself from that situation immediately.

Having a "go to" phrase that has been practiced will help diffuse the situation. It can be "Let's talk about this later," "We'll meet again on this," or "I need to walk away right now."

Come up with your own phrase that is comfortable to say, and practice it before you need it. The main thing is to get out of there before things escalate. Don't try to reason with an angry employee. End the meeting. Nothing will be accomplished when one or both parties feel strong emotions.

Before you meet again, review your assumptions. Have you looked at the situation from their side? Why did they get angry? What buttons did you push? Were you polite and professional?

The next time you meet, you may want to have another

person in the room, maybe even someone from the human resources department. If things get heated again, you will want to have a witness.

The employee has a responsibility to accept negative news from their supervisor and follow the directives to correct the situation. But you want to understand what caused their emotions to run high.

You can start the new conversation with "I need your help understanding what happened the last time we met. Can you give me your perspective of that conversation?"

Find out where they are coming from, so that you can understand their viewpoint before continuing the difficult conversation that still needs to be had.

GIVING BAD NEWS

There are times you will need to have conversations to break bad news to your employees—such as terminations, layoffs, and corrective actions. These will be difficult for you, but even more difficult for the recipient.

First, don't delay. Have the conversation as soon as you can.

Next, help them prepare to receive bad news. Don't start

with small talk or chit-chat. Let them know right away that bad news is coming, with phrases like "This is awkward..." "There is no easy way to say this..." or "I have some news that may be hard for you to hear..."

Don't hedge on the information you are giving. Use succinct, direct terms. Don't say, "I feel that you..." "You might have..." "It appears..." or "It seems..."

Acknowledge their grief after you give the bad news. Offer such phrases as, "I know this is hard for you." "Go ahead and take a moment." "When you are ready, we'll continue."

Don't make it about you. I had a friend who was part of a departmental layoff. By the time she was called in to her boss's office, she knew what was coming and she tried to make a joke about it to mask her own nervousness. Her boss snapped at her and said, "Don't make this any harder for me! This is a very stressful day!" Needless to say, the stressful day was really on the part of my friend, who was now unemployed.

As a leader, you can't avoid difficult conversations.

But if you deal with these issues quickly and get things back on track, it's all part of a learning process.

KEY TAKEAWAYS

- Use the SAS method for having an uncomfortable or difficult conversation with an employee: **S**ee the situation from the employee's view, **A**ssume the employee had positive intent, **S**cript and practice for the discussion.

- Describe the behavior, the effect on the organization or department, and the expected behavior in the future.

- There is no place for anger in the workplace. Be ready with phrases to remove yourself from the situation when anger flares.

- To give bad news, use a short phrase to let them know bad news is coming, give them the news, and then allow them their grief.

CHAPTER 10

"HOW AM I DOING?"

USING FEEDBACK EFFECTIVELY

Make feedback normal. Not a performance review.

—ED BATISTA

Do you get enough feedback from your boss? Likely your answer is "no."

Do you give your employees enough feedback? Bet you said "yes!"

Data shows that 58 percent of supervisors said they provide enough feedback, but only 35 percent of all employees feel they get enough feedback.[8]

---

8 "Employee Feedback: The Complete Guide," Officevibe, accessed September 9, 2019, https://www.officevibe.com/employee-engagement-solution/employee-feedback.

So you are probably not giving feedback as often as you think.

Feedback is defined as transmitting information back to the original source about an action, which is used as a basis for improvement. It's all about future actions and improvement.

CHECK-IN WITH ROGER

Our friend Roger avoided giving feedback to his employees. Positive or negative, it didn't matter—the subject was avoided. Why? Because he didn't know how it would be received or what it would accomplish. An employee may get mad at him for negative feedback. Or they could brag to their friends if they received positive feedback, and that could cause jealousy among the staff. Feedback wasn't given to Roger by his own boss, so he had no model for it. It seemed like it was more trouble than it was worth.

IMPORTANT TO EMPLOYEE ENGAGEMENT

Providing positive and negative feedback on a regular basis is an important element of engaging employees. Feedback enhances the supervisor/employee relationship. It also helps the employee grow, both personally and professionally.

In fact, feedback could be considered one of the top steps a supervisor can take to increase an employee's engagement, second only to the weekly "See, I See You" meetings with their supervisor (chapter 1).

Feedback, if given well, has an immediate "bang for the buck." It is the simplest way to make changes in employee performance and behavior.

Ed Batista, author and executive coach, says, "To become more effective and fulfilled at work, people need a keen understanding of their impact on others and the extent to which they're achieving their goals in their working relationships. Direct feedback is the most efficient way for them to gather this information and learn from it."

Many supervisors, like Roger, avoid giving feedback—or if they do, it is criticism after a big mistake the employee makes.

Properly given and timed, feedback should just be a small adjustment or pat on the back for a small error or accomplishment. Consider it a *micro intervention.*

If feedback is held until something big happens, there is the risk of costly mistakes, or missed opportunities to slowly guide the employee back on track, or to encourage good behavior to continue.

FEEDBACK SANDWICH—DON'T FEED THEM DONUTS AND SARDINES

A commonly held belief on negative feedback is that it should be "sandwiched" between two pieces of positive feedback, to "soften" the blow. This process has been compared to making a sardine sandwich with donuts! The end result is not "softened"—it's "soggy" and not effective.

It's human nature—the recipient will focus on the two positives and downplay the negative.

Let the negative feedback stand on its own. Your urge to soften it is to avoid your own discomfort, but that is not helpful for the employee who needs to hear the direct truth.

Get comfortable with frequent micro bits of feedback— positive and negative—with each being given in their own time to be the most effective.

Feedback should be like those roadside electric signs that reflect your speed back to you. In fact, the official name for those are "driver feedback" signs.

This is how you should handle your feedback to your employee.

It's not a big deal—you are just reflecting their behavior back to them, letting them know the effect it had and setting an expectation for the future. It is shining a mirror back onto them, so they can see their actions and the impact.

WHAT TO SAY

Like other uncomfortable conversations, it's best to have a script that you practice ahead of time. Use the same words, demeanor, and tone of voice whether you are giving positive or negative feedback.

The point of feedback is to change future behavior. In fact, if it didn't affect behavior in the future, there would be no need to give feedback. You can't change the past. But, if you want your staff to continue to do the good stuff and stop doing the bad stuff, you have to tell them.

Here are the steps to giving feedback—both negative and positive:

1. Ask permission: "May I give you some feedback?"
2. Describe the behavior and explain the impact: "When you do X, it causes Y."
3. Define future behavior: "In the future, please do Z."

Here is an example of negative feedback that Roger might give:

Roger: "Sofia, could I give you some feedback?"

Sofia: "I guess so."

Roger: "When you don't put enough documentation in your patient-care report, it gets kicked out of the system and causes a billing delay. In the future, please take a couple of extra minutes to make sure it is complete."

Sofia's reaction is up to her. She may say, "Okay," or seem irritated or even get angry. But that doesn't change the fact that Roger has given her the information in a direct and professional way.

If Sofia does not accept the feedback in the same professional way, that is a topic for a future session at a weekly meeting. It's part of an employee's job to accept feedback from their boss. Refusal to accept it or to make the changes requested is a performance issue.

Here is an example of positive feedback from Roger:

Roger: "Tad, could I give you some feedback?"

Tad: "Sure."

Roger: "When you get to work early to make sure the ambulance is stocked before your shift, it really helps the dispatch center get set up for the changeover. Keep up the good work!"

No matter whether the feedback is positive or negative, maintain a neutral tone of voice. This may take some practicing until it feels normal, but having a script will help.

Make the feedback conversation short and sweet, with no sign of emotion or frustration. Then move on.

When giving feedback, assume the employee wants to do the right thing. This is an important part of all uncomfortable conversations. We need to assume that they did not mean to make a mistake or cause a problem, so we are just helping them notice it so they can adjust and not do it again. If the problem continues, then they may not have positive intent and then it is time to go down a corrective action road.

WHY ASK PERMISSION?

By asking permission, you are making sure the employee is ready to hear the feedback. They might be having a bad day or had something happen at home that has them distracted, or they may be too busy to absorb the information.

Respect a "no" and let them come back to you later to see what you were going to say. If they don't come back to you, let it go. If they repeat the behavior, you will provide feedback on the new behavior. If they never do it again, then you didn't need to have the discussion, because the purpose of feedback is to change future behavior.

If you get a second "no" the next time you try to give feedback, then it is time to discuss the reason for their refusals at their next meeting.

Also, make sure you are in the proper mindset to give the feedback. If you are having a bad day, it might be better to wait until tomorrow. You need to be prepared to deliver the feedback with no emotion.

TIMING

You should give feedback whenever you see a behavior that needs adjusting or encouraging. Feedback should be given as soon as possible after the event. If you are unable to give the feedback within two days, let it go. If the behavior repeats, you can give feedback then. If it doesn't repeat, then you're good.

You should give positive feedback more often than negative. Since we often associate feedback as negative, you may have to make an effort to look for opportunities to find your staff doing something well. At a minimum, find something to give positive feedback on for each employee at least once per week.

"Employees who report receiving recognition and praise within the last seven days show increased productivity, get higher scores from customers, and have better safety records. They're just more engaged at work," says Tom Rath of *Strengths Based Leadership*.

Feedback should be given privately. Even positive feedback given in front of coworkers can backfire and make the employee uncomfortable.

Timing is important, especially for negative feedback. Sometimes immediately after the situation is too soon, but more than two days later can be too late.

Simon botched up a presentation at a meeting. He was upset and embarrassed afterward. Simon knows he messed up. His boss let him have some time to himself, and the next day went to his office to ask, "Hey, want to talk about yesterday's presentation?"

Simon says, "I'm beating myself up about it."

So, this may not be the time for Simon's boss to use his script: "When you botched up the presentation, it reflected poorly on the organization, and we lost the account. Next time, practice the presentation in front of me so that you can be successful." Simon already knows the effects and is giving himself plenty of negative feedback, so his boss may want to take a step back and let Simon give himself his own script. The boss's role should just be supportive at that point.

In his book *Work Rules*, Google HR Executive Laslo Bock says, "For any open position, Google will be interrogating 100 people simultaneously. After six weeks of this, 99 are rejected." They're not told why. "If somebody just breaks up with you," Bock says, "that's not the time to hear: 'And really, next time, send more flowers.'...For the most part people actually aren't excited to get that feedback, because they really wanted the job. They argue. They're not in a place where they can learn."

To accept feedback, make sure your staff are in a place where they can learn.

Once you get comfortable with your script and giving feedback to your staff, ask your boss to give you more frequent feedback. And, if he doesn't know how—give him the script!

KEY TAKEAWAYS

- Feedback is one of the most effective skills for engaging employees.

- The purpose of feedback is to mold future behavior.

- Both positive and negative feedback should be given with scripted words.

- Look for opportunities to give more positive than negative feedback.

CHAPTER 11

"DELEGATION IS AN EDUCATION"

SHARE THE WORK TO DEVELOP THE EMPLOYEE

If you delegate tasks, you create followers. If you delegate authority, you create leaders.

—CRAIG GROESCHEL

CHECK-IN WITH ROGER

In our story of Roger, he would rather do the work himself to make sure it gets done right. This is the most common reason supervisors give for not delegating.

Delegation is one of the hardest parts of the Engagement Ring.

WHY IS DELEGATING SO HARD?

Delegating means turning over a responsibility for a project or task to one of your employees. However, supervisors tend to shy away from doing this. The reasons are varied. Like Roger, they may not trust their employees' commitment, interest, or ability to do the job right.

Managers may also feel that it takes too much time to train and supervise the employee performing the task, or the supervisor may actually like to do those duties themselves. There may be guilt associated with giving more work to overworked employees. Some supervisors might also have a need to make themselves indispensable, so that no one else can do their job.

Other supervisors are proud of the fact that they won't ask their staff to do anything they wouldn't do. They like to show they can "roll up their sleeves" and work alongside the staff. This can be admirable for the short term when there is a project that requires all-hands-on-deck, but it is not the measure of an effective manager in the long run.

"The inability to delegate is one of the biggest problems I see with managers at all levels," says Eli Broad in *The Art of Being Unreasonable: Lessons in Unconventional Thinking.* "Find the best people to whom you can delegate, and know their strengths and weaknesses. If you think you can do it better, delegate anyway and try as hard as you can to close that gap by giving your colleague or employee the right feedback. Then recognize and accept that just because someone does something a little differently than you would, that doesn't mean it's wrong. What counts is that your goals get accomplished at a sufficient level of quality."

BENEFITS OF DELEGATING

You should delegate for the following reasons:

- Develop and stretch your staff so they can learn new skills
- Test your staff and develop trust in their abilities
- They come up with new ways to do tasks
- Free yourself from lower-level tasks and projects so you can take on some of your boss's projects and grow yourself

Delegation maximizes the output of a department! You and your staff can accomplish more when the work is divided, and your staff will be more engaged when they are given stretch assignments.

By some estimates, the average person is said to only work

at 50 percent capacity. Effective delegating can tap the other 50 percent to increase an employee's productivity.

Look at your projects and tasks. What could be moved to someone else? Who could do it cheaper? Who might be able to do it better?

Think through the abilities, talents, and interests of your staff. Match the project to the person. Start small to test it out. As the employees show their abilities, move more complex tasks to them.

Perhaps you have levels of staff. The lower levels could be delegated work from the level above, until the level just below you has the ability to take on some of your tasks or projects.

TEN-STEP PROCESS FOR DELEGATING

Step 1: Set up a list of projects and tasks that could be delegated. Sort them by complexity.

Step 2: Rank your employees by their abilities to handle complex tasks.

Step 3: Match a task to an employee. Delegate less complex tasks to newer employees to build their confidence and abilities.

Step 4: Meet with the employee to tell them about the task and why they were chosen. Ask them if they are willing to take on the new assignment. Be accepting of those who may turn it down.

Step 5: For those staff willing to take on the assignment, be specific about the deadlines, quality measures, and outcomes. Be clear about what level of authority they have. Responsibility without authority does not set the employee up for success.

Step 6: Set up a schedule for milestones, deadlines, and progress meetings. Progress check-ins may take place at the weekly "See, I See You" meetings (see chapter 1).

Step 7: Meet, discuss, give feedback, and be supportive.

Step 8: When the project has been completed, have a debriefing session to discuss lessons learned.

Step 9: Be sure to celebrate and congratulate!

Step 10: Repeat with more complex tasks and projects.

ANTICIPATE BUMPS IN THE ROAD

There will be a learning curve, so expect that it will take your staff more time than it takes you to complete the task or project. Be prepared for errors, but set up a culture where mistakes are just considered learning experiences, not punished.

If you are uncomfortable, start to delegate just the simplest tasks and see how that goes.

To delegate, you must be prepared to be held responsible for something that you cannot control. If you don't get comfortable with that, you won't be able to do it consistently or well.

As Booker T. Washington said, "Few things can help an individual more than to place responsibility on him, and to let him know you trust him."

And, as Ronald Reagan said, "Trust, but verify."

Delegating is a skill that will get easier the more you do it. Practice makes perfect.

NOT EVERYONE WANTS TO CLIMB THE LADDER

When asking an employee to accept a stretch assignment, honor a "no." Staff members may not feel ready, may already feel overworked, or may have some fears about taking on more responsibilities. Encourage them to discuss their reasons.

Delegation should not be mandatory. If the tasks and projects are a requirement of their job, then it is not truly a delegation of higher-level duties. If the higher-level tasks and projects are not in their job description, then accepting the delegated work should be optional.

Don't force stretch assignments if they don't want it. Not everyone will want or can handle this type of growth. Meet them where they are as employees, and help them get to where they aspire to be. Not every employee wants to be promoted up the career ladder.

My father was a hardworking, family man. A second-generation American who fought in WWII and took advantage of the GI bill to be the first in his family to go to college, he became a mechanical engineer. He was hired straight out of college by General Motors Corporation and soon rose up the engineering ranks at their Detroit headquarters, working alongside John DeLorean (of the wing-door car fame).

When Dad's abilities got him promoted to a management position, he became unhappy. He felt more experienced employees had been bypassed—and now he was their supervisor. And, to top it off, he was no longer doing the hands-on engineering work that he loved, but instead was supervising those doing that work.

The situation came to a head when my dad saw a notice posted on the employee bulletin board inviting non-management staff to a weekend lake outing. In big letters on the invitation were the words in the 1950s vernacular that changed my dad's career path, "No Chiefs, Only Indians."

The sign summed up all his negative feelings about the promotion. He felt the sting of not belonging, lacking the "I" of being included, and felt the loss of friendships after his promotion (some of the topics discussed in chapters 2 and 3). He came home from work and informed my mother that he was going to find another job where he could just be an "Indian"—one of the guys, just doing the engineering work that he loved. And, so he did—finding a job back in their hometown, with Dad happily walking in the door from work every evening at 5:30 on the dot and working until retirement as an engineer, doing the work he loved and never again supervising an employee.

AVOID MICROMANAGING

Micromanaging is defined as "to manage or control with excessive attention to minor details."

There is a difference between being supportive and being a micromanager. Don't jump in to fix problems, but rather coach employees through finding the answers (see chapter 6 for coaching tips). Be prepared to offer extra time and patience in this delegation process.

SOMETIMES YOU HAVE TO LET IT GO

If your staff feels you are going to swoop in and change their work or take over and do it yourself, they will not be motivated to take on any stretch assignments the next time.

At the boutique where Connie works, the owners wanted to delegate and empower some of the most senior employees with a project. They decided to form a committee with those senior employees and give them the responsibility for recommending which of the junior staff would receive an incentive based on specific guidelines provided by the owners.

The committee met, decided on, and submitted their recommendations. The owners reviewed the recommendations, ignored them, and decided on the recipients themselves.

This did more harm than if they had never delegated the project in the first place. The committee felt they had wasted their time, that their opinions didn't matter, and, worse yet, that the owners had not fairly given out the incentives based on the criteria that the owners themselves had set.

If you are going to delegate, be prepared that you may not agree with the way the work was done, but also be prepared to decide if the difference is worth overriding the employee who put in the effort.

In the case of the boutique, the incentives were gift cards of a nominal amount, and even if they had been given to whom the owners thought were the "wrong" employees, it would not have been much of a financial hardship on the boutique. Plus, they would have had the value of a happy committee and some happy employees who received the gift cards. As it turned out, word got around the shop of how it was handled by the owners, and even the recipients that the owners chose for the incentives were disenchanted with the process by the time they received their gift cards.

It's hard to let go of control. Yes, you know how to do the task or project better than your employee. But, maybe not. Maybe your employee will bring some insight or a new way to do the task. Even if they don't, they will learn, grow, and develop in doing it.

At first, you will spend more time making sure deadlines and goals are met. But soon, you (and Roger) will have the time to be able to ask for some stretch assignments for yourselves!

KEY TAKEAWAYS

- Delegate to grow your employees, stretch their skills, take work off your plate, and leverage the output of the department.

- When delegating, match your employees' strengths, skills, and interests to the tasks. Find something to delegate to staff at every level, and move to more complex tasks as their abilities develop.

- Delegation should not be mandatory—always ask.

- Avoid micromanaging the task, and let go of control. Your staff may just surprise you!

CHAPTER 12

"BLOOM WHERE YOU ARE PLANTED"

CULTIVATING AND GROWING STAFF

He who would fly one day must first learn to stand and walk and run and climb and dance; one cannot fly into flying.

—FRIEDRICH NIETZSCHE

GETTING YOUR GARDEN TO FLOURISH

How important is it for you to be able to personally and professionally develop on the job?

Gallup statistics show that 87 percent of millennial-aged employees say that the opportunity to learn and grow is one of the top-three reasons to stay in a job.[9] But, guess what? Only 39 percent said they had learned something in the last thirty days that would help them do their job better.

The last piece of the Engagement Ring is "G" for growing. Other studies have also shown that opportunities for personal and professional growth at work lead to increased engagement among employees of all ages.

We have already talked about helping staff grow and develop using feedback, delegation, coaching, team building, goals, and measurement. All of these can result in personal and professional development.

The missing piece is proactive steps that employees can take to develop themselves—and that you, as their leader, can do to help and support them. The employee needs to direct the journey, but you can provide opportunities and support. Be their champion! Help them pinpoint where their interests are and what they hope to accomplish.

Bryan Chenault is the director of human resources at Whitlock. He encourages his employees to take an hour every week for personal development. In fact, he wants

---

9   Amy Adkins and Brandon Rigoni, "Millennials Want Jobs to Be Development Opportunities," Gallup, August 7, 2019, https://www.gallup.com/workplace/236438/millennials-jobs-development-opportunities.aspx.

them to put it on their calendars. "I tell them to block off an hour to develop somehow—reading articles, taking webinars, watching TED Talks, reading books, or even taking a break away from their work to let their creative juices flow. Encouraging them to take an hour a week for their own development benefits our team and the organization overall. Even if they don't use that hour every week, just knowing I encourage it demonstrates how important I consider it to be and that they can take advantage of it anytime they like."

Showing support to the staff for developmental opportunities, whether encouraging them to block off time on the calendar like Bryan or pulling the staff together for a workshop, shows them that you are committed to their development.

John C. Maxwell said, "Growth is the great separator between those who succeed and those who do not. When I see a person beginning to separate themselves from the pack, it's almost always due to personal growth."

What is the difference between personal and professional growth? They can overlap, intermingle, and be pretty much the same thing. Developing personal skills, such as a staff member working on their emotional intelligence, will benefit their job. Developing professional skills, such as returning to college to finish their degree, will also result in personal growth.

WATERING AND FERTILIZING

What steps can you take to help your staff grow?

Individual Coaching: Make personal and professional development a topic at their weekly "See, I See You" meetings. (Not having those? See chapter 1.)

Work on formalizing plans for development for each employee—for the next thirty days, ninety days, quarter, six months, and/or the year. Help them visualize where they want to be in their development in the future (see chapter 6 for coaching skills), and then help them work backward to detail the steps to get there. This could be an annual event at the beginning of the calendar or fiscal year or take place at their performance evaluation. The questions you should be asking are "Where do you see yourself in the future? And how can I help you get there?"

Sharing with the Team: Having team members share their learning and development plans at a staff meeting would be a great way to motivate the team. Having staff prepare a short update or lesson every time they have a new learning opportunity reinforces their learning and increases learning and development of the whole team.

Developing Their Leadership Abilities: Maybe your employee's goal is to obtain a supervisory position, and you can provide them with opportunities to lead a team. Maybe they are interested in developing some digital skills, and you can arrange for a stint in the IT department. Find out what interests them outside of their current job.

Completing Their Degree: For an employee who wants to return to school, does the company have a tuition reimbursement plan? If not, maybe you can support them by adjusting their time schedule so they can attend classes.

Offer Developmental Activities: Bring in outside speakers or experts to present at staff meetings, lunch-and-learns, or professional-development seminars and workshops.

Budget for It: Include an amount per staff member per year in the annual budget for development, so that you can send staff offsite to classes and training that will help them reach their goals.

Create a Book Club: At Neil's staff meeting, leadership books were randomly laid out in front of each seat. Staff were invited to sit wherever they chose. At the end of the meeting, Neil instructed them that the book in front of them was theirs to read and keep, but that they were to get together with others in the meeting who had the same book. They were to read the book and do a group book report, with a summary and the key points of the book, to be presented as a group at the next month's meeting. Many of the staff members had never read a leadership book before, but they were surprisingly enthusiastic a month later to share what they had learned with the rest of the staff. The key to this is to allow—and in fact, make mandatory—reading the book and preparing the book report during work hours. Let them know that you consider professional development as important as the daily responsibilities of their job.

Have Peer Mentor Program: Assign experienced staff members to mentor new staff members. During a Leadership Academy program, Keisha had each newly promoted management staff member assigned to a mentor from the leadership staff. The duo was given an amount of money to go out to lunch to get to know each other. Then they were encouraged to meet regularly and develop their mentor/mentee relationship for a year. After a year, the mentee was assigned to be a mentor to a new leader. This was a developmental opportunity for both the mentor and mentee. The staff might not necessarily be on the same level, as a new director could be assigned a mentor who was on a supervisor level, but the mentor had been in the leadership group longer and welcomed the new member and showed them the ropes.

CHECK-IN WITH ROGER

What could our friend Roger do to encourage professional and personal development with his team? The paramedics already had requirements for continuing education credits to keep their certifications up to date, and these classes were provided by the agency.

But, they were millennials, and the statistics show that most want to learn, grow, and develop in other ways.

During his weekly "See, I See You" meetings, Roger should be finding out about his staff's goals.

With the physical requirements of being a paramedic, it was rare to find a staff member continuing this line of work over the age of forty. Knowing that the career can be physically limiting, Roger needs to have honest conversations with the staff about what their next steps would be in their career. From there, opportunities to develop the staff members could be found, promoted, and supported.

Diane wants to go to nursing school. Raul wants to go back to college and get a degree in business. Anita wants to go into training, to develop the next generation of EMS professionals.

Roger should track each employee's goals on a spreadsheet. He should share the spreadsheet with his boss and human resources to find out which developmental opportunities might be available within the organization or could be sponsored.

HOW ABOUT YOU?

How important is personal and professional development to you? What are you doing to grow yourself?

Make the time to develop yourself, and model the behavior you want to see in your staff.

KEY TAKEAWAYS

- Opportunities for personal and professional growth at work benefit the employee and the organization.

- Meet with each employee about how they want to grow.

- Formalize plans, and track and monitor progress for each staff member.

- Group growth opportunities can include workshops, lunch-and-learns, book clubs, and peer mentor programs.

CONCLUSION

When the story is ready to be told, it will write itself.

—UNKNOWN

All the elements came together, and here it is.

Developing relationships, making your staff feel they belong, connecting them to the mission, and helping them grow will set you on the path to be a successful leader, with engaged, productive, and fulfilled employees.

All the parts of the Engagement Ring have been summarized for you in a graphic, and there is a checklist at the end of this book to keep you on track. Now go forth and engage.

But wait, what about you? Are you engaged yourself?

Employees who work for highly engaged managers are 59 percent more likely to be engaged.[10] So, it's going to be hard for you to increase engagement in your staff if you don't feel it yourself.

All employees should have the opportunity to be engaged at work, no matter what their job level. Even "C" suite leaders want to be known by their supervisor, be in the loop, be coached, be connected to the mission, and receive feedback and stretch opportunities.

If you are not receiving these things from your boss, you know what to ask for now that you've read the book.

The Engagement Ring is a story that wrote itself.

I hope Roger reads it.

10 DeAnn Wandler, "The Role of Management in Employee Engagement,"
    Main, August 1, 2019, https://www.td.org/magazines/the-public-manager/
    the-role-of-management-in-employee-engagement.

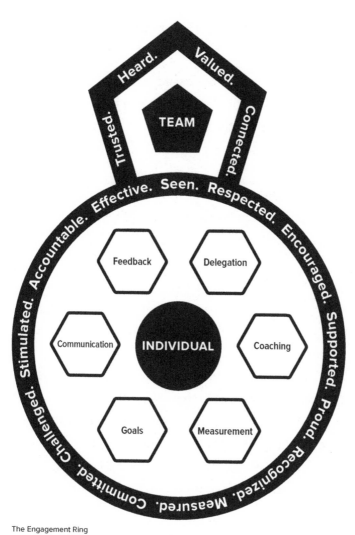

The Engagement Ring

EMPLOYEE ENGAGEMENT CHECKLIST

RELATIONSHIPS

- ☐ I know my employees as individuals.
- ☐ I make my employees feel known by showing a genuine interest in them.
- ☐ I show respect to my staff and help them to succeed at work.
- ☐ I encourage and inspire my team to do their best work.
- ☐ I support my employees by providing them access to what they need to do their job well.

INCLUDED

- ☐ I demonstrate an interest in my employees' well-being.
- ☐ I make sure my employees feel heard by valuing and encouraging them to share their opinions.
- ☐ I foster belonging in my employees by showing them the value they bring to the team.
- ☐ I connect with my employees by keeping them informed about what is happening in our organization.
- ☐ I trust my employees and know they are an important member of our team.

NEEDED

- ☐ I made my staff feel important by showing them how their job moves the organization's mission forward.
- ☐ I want my employees to feel proud and to recommend our company as a great place to work.
- ☐ I recognize my employees by providing positive feedback when they do good work.
- ☐ I provide systems for measurement, so my employees always know what their goals and objectives are.
- ☐ I believe in our company's mission and foster commitment in my staff to promote the mission.

GROWING

- ☐ I provide feedback, challenging assignments, and training for my employees' personal and professional growth.
- ☐ I help develop my staff by providing them with a clear understanding of their career path.
- ☐ I recognize my staff's full potential and capitalize on their strengths.
- ☐ I let my team know what is expected of them and hold them accountable.
- ☐ I foster a feeling of effectiveness in my team by showing them how their work affects the overall success of the company.

ACKNOWLEDGMENTS

With love and gratitude to those who cheered me on this path to writing a book:

My daughters and their families: Jenn, Brad, and Zoë Nixon; Jessye and Ken (and rescue dogs) Michaels; and Emily, Shaun, and Charlotte Smith. I felt their love and support through every step of the process.

My sister, Karen Szkutnik, who understands the leadership concepts I was trying to impart and was my sounding board as I put them together.

My friend, Martha Bendl, who never failed to check in to see how the book was going.

My mother, Bernie Weihs, who is my biggest cheerleader and inspiration.

And last, but not least, my husband, Steve Pond, whose enthusiasm for this project and unwavering love and support made it possible to accomplish.

RESOURCES

Blank, Pete. *Employee Engagement: Lessons from the Mouse House.* Pete Blank, 2012.

Bungay Stanier, Michael. *The Coaching Habit: Say Less, Ask More & Change the Way You Lead Forever.* Toronto, Canada: Box of Crayons Press, 2016.

Caraher, Lee. *The Boomerang Principle: Inspire Lifetime Loyalty From Your Employees.* Abington, Oxon: UK. Taylor & Francis Group, LLC, 2017.

Finnegan, Richard P. *Raise Your Team's Employee Engagement Score: A Manager's Guide.* New York, NY: Richard P. Finnegan, 2018.

Genett, Donna M., Ph.D. *If You Want It Done Right, You Don't Have to Do It Yourself!: The Power of Effective Delegation.* Fresno, CA: Linden Publishing, 2004.

Goleman, Daniel. *Emotional Intelligence.* New York, NY: Bantam Books, 1995.

Horstman, Mark. *The Effective Manager.* Hoboken, NJ: Manager Tools Publishing, 2016.

Lencioni, Patrick. *The Truth About Employee Engagement: A Fable About Addressing the Three Root Causes of Job Misery.* San Francisco, CA: Jossey-Bass, 2007.

Logan, David and King, John. *Tribal Leadership.* New York, NY: HarperCollins, 2008.

McCoy, Thomas J. *15 Essential Questions (and Answers) That Ensure Successful Engagement: A Group Discussion Handbook.* Thomas J. McCoy, 2018.

Neitlich, Andrew. *The Way to Coach: Leaders, Executives, and Managers.* Sarasota, FL: The Center for Executive Coaching, 2016.

Stein, Scott. *Leadership Hacks: Clever Shortcuts to Boost Your Impact and Results.* Milton, Qld Australia: John Wiley & Sons Australia Ltd, 2018.

Bariso. *13 Things Emotionally Intelligent People Do.* https://www.inc.com/justin-bariso/13-things-emotionally-intelligent-people-do.html.

Batista-Taran, L. C., Shuck, M. B., Gutierrez, C. C., & Baralt, S. (2009). The Role of Leadership Style in Employee Engagement. In M. S. Plakhotnik, S. M. Nielsen, & D. M. Pane (eds.), Proceedings of the Eighth Annual College of Education & GSN Research Conference (pp. 15-20). Miami: Florida International University. http://coeweb.fiu.edu/research_conference/.

Blanchard & Blanchard. (2011). Do Your People Really Know What You Expect of Them? https://www.fastcompany.com/1767714/do-your-people-really-know-what-you-expect-them.

Bradberry. (2018). Ten Communication *Secrets* of Great Leaders. https://www.inc.com/travis-bradberry/10-communication-secrets-of-great-leaders.html.

Casserly. (2012). Majority of Americans Would Rather Fire Their Boss than Get a Raise. https://www.forbes.com/sites/meghancasserly/2012/10/17/majority-of-americans-would-rather-fire-their-boss-than-get-a-raise/#5c8e9f746610.

Culture Amp. (2018). Diversity, Inclusion and Intersectionality. https://cdn2.hubspot.net/hubfs/516278/cultureamp-diversity-inclusion-2018.pdf.

Culture Amp. 6 Ways to Foster Belonging in the Workplace: Taking Diversity & Inclusion to the Next Level. https://hello.cultureamp.com/hubfs/1703-Belonging/Culture-Amp_6-ways-to-foster-belonging.pdf.

Harter. (2019). 5 Questions Every Onboarding Program Must Answer. https://www.gallup.com/workplace/247598/questions-every-onboarding-program-answer.aspx.

Hills. (2018). How an Understanding of Neuroscience Can Help Inclusion. https://headheartbrain.com/resources/how-an-understanding-of-neuroscience-can-help-create-inclusion/.

Holtzclaw. (2013). 5 Things Smart Managers Know about Building Teams. https://www.inc.com/eric-v-holtzclaw/5-things-smart-managers-know-about-building-teams.html.

Huppert. (2017). Employees Share What Gives Them a Sense of Belonging at Work. https://business.linkedin.com/talent-solutions/blog/company-culture/2017/employees-share-what-gives-them-a-sense-of-belonging-at-work.

Johnson. (2016). 6 Steps to Build a Strong Team. https://www.entrepreneur.com/article/274001.

Lavoie. (2017). How to Engage Employees through Your Company Vision Statement. https://www.entrepreneur.com/article/290803.

Kulpa. (2017). How to Prevent Disengaged Employees from Killing Your Bottom Line. https://www.entrepreneur.com/article/305506.

Lloyd. (2019). Managers Must Delegate Effectively to Develop Employees. https://www.shrm.org/resourcesandtools/hr-topics/organizational-and-employee-development/pages/delegateeffectively.aspx.

Mann. (2018). Why We Need Best Friends at Work. https://www.gallup.com/workplace/236213/why-need-best-friends-work.aspx.

McLoed. (2018). Maslow's Hierarchy of Needs. https://www.simplypsychology.org/maslow.html.

Mills. (2019). Storytelling to Captivate, Engage, and Influence. https://www.td.org/insights/storytelling-to-captivate-engage-and-influence.

Milner. (2018). Most Managers Don't Know How to Coach People but They Can Learn. https://hbr.org/2018/08/most-managers-dont-know-how-to-coach-people-but-they-can-learn.

Novak. (2019). Leadership Communication: Learn It, Prioritize It, Be Successful. https://learn.g2.com/leadership-communication.

Oehler, Stomski, Kustra-Olszewska. (2014). What Makes Someone an Engaging Leader. https://hbr.org/2014/11/what-makes-someone-an-engaging-leader.

Reilly. Five Ways to Improve Employee Engagement Now. https://www.gallup.com/workplace/231581/five-ways-improve-employee-engagement.aspx.

Reilly. (2017). How LinkedIn HR Chief Is Changing Diversity Conversation with "Belonging." https://business.linkedin.com/talent-solutions/blog/diversity/2017/how-linkedins-hr-chief-is-changing-the-diversity-conversation-with-belonging.

Rigoni and Nelson. (2016). Millenials Not Connecting with Their Company's Mission. https://www.gallup.com/workplace/236342/millennials-not-connecting-company-mission.aspx.

Sostrin. (2017). To Be a Great Leader, You Have to Learn How to Delegate Well. https://hbr.org/2017/10/to-be-a-great-leader-you-have-to-learn-how-to-delegate-well.

Wang. (2015). Why You Must Support Coworker Friendships for Employee Engagement. https://www.tinypulse.com/blog/why-you-must-support-coworker-friendships-for-employee-engagement.

Wadors. (2016). The Power of Belonging. https://www.youtube.com/watch?v=xwadscBnlhU.

Made in the USA
Monee, IL
19 February 2023

28220791R00111